Title of this book

Hinduism (Sanatan Dharma) - A Practical Manual for the Enthusiastic Novice.

Brief description of this book

This book covers the topics of Hinduism (Sanatan Dharma) in general. It gives a brief resume of its books, talks about one God, introduces some of its central symbols, highlights the importance of AUM (OM), outline the role of the demigods (devatas) and the nine (nav) planets (grahas),make known the three (traya) bodies (shariras) and the five (panch) sheaths (koshas), provide information about The Lord,prakrti-maya-gunas and the individual; it presents an insight on the living embodied being (jiva), explain pathways to experiencing the self (Aatma), emphasizes the role of the mind and Hindu (Sanatanist) calendar in preparation for experiencing one's real nature i.e, the soul (Aatma) which is absolute (samagram) existence (Sat), absolute (samagram) consciousness/awareness (Chit) and absolute (samagram) bliss (Anandam).

Reasons for this book

As a practising Hindu (Sanatanist), I very humbly inform its readership, that my knowledge of this ancient religion of ours was very poor up to the time of preparing this manuscript; there were numerous occasions in my life, when I was asked to explain it to others, alas, my knowledge was found wanting.

My motivation for writing this book was to utilise it as a learning tool, to add to my fund of knowledge, so that it can inform my practice. During the course of my journey through life, I met many individuals whose predicament was the same as mine. This book is for this group as well.

The target audience for this book

This book is aimed at those who want to:
1) Learn about Hinduism (Sanatan Dharma).
2) Utilise it to enrich the quality of their lifestyles.
3) Commence on the pathway to enhance their spiritual growth.

Lessons learnt from writing this book

1) Anything is possible with the grace of The Lord.
2) This body-mind-intellect (ksetram) is temporary but the soul   (Aatma) is timeless.
3) To maximise each day and dedicate each piece of action as a service to The Lord.

Foreword

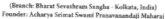

BHARAT SEVASHRAM SANGHA CANADA

(Branch: Bharat Sevashram Sangha - Kolkata, India)
Founder: Acharya Srimat Swami Pranavanandaji Maharaj

December 15, 2016

A WELCOME ADDITION FOR THE PROPAGATION OF HINDUISM

There is already an obvious plethora of authoritative texts on various aspects of Hinduism. Many of these have been written by acknowledged experts and researchers in the limitless field of religion and philosophy; however, it is not often that we come across a virtual 'handbook' for the understanding and practice of our Dharma like this volume written by a devotee such as our dear brother, Raikha Bisnath Tiwari whose antecedents were well-known, highly respected, practicing Pandits in Guyana and whose pragmatic examples must have had a major influence on Raikhaji's head and hands and which finally culminated in his writing this useful text.

I have been afforded the privilege and pleasure of pre-viewing Raikhaji's work and now have no hesitation in strongly recommending it to all potential readers, Hindus and non-Hindus alike who are in search of more knowledge and understanding of our live and limitless religion. Of Sri Raikha's manual on Hinduism, it is a "Reflections of the Past and sustainability for the future".

With sincere thanks to Bhai RaikhaJi for his continuing yeoman's service to our Sanatan Dharma.

Swami Bhajanananda
Bharat Sevashram Sangha -Canada
(Pranav Hindu Heritage and Cultural Centre)

102 Rivalda Road, Toronto, Ontario M9M 2M8   Tel: (416) 741-4335 • Fax: (416) 744-6305

HEAD OFFICE: Bharat Sevashram Sangha, 211 Rash Behari Avenue, Kolkata - 19, India
BRANCHES: Delhi, Brindavan, Kurukshetra, Gujarat - Ahmedabad, Surat, Dwarka, Mumbai, Haridwar, Varanasi, Badrinath, Kedarnath, Rameshwaram, Kanyakumari, Ghatsila, Jamshedpur, Jammu, etc. OVERSEAS: London, U.S.A., Canada, Trinidad, Guyana, Fiji, etc.

Acknowledgements

I gratefully, sincerely and humbly acknowledge The Grace of Lord Ganesh, who blessed me with the will and motivation to write this book.

Lord Ganesh enriched my life, with several wonderful and empathic human beings, whose love, guidance and support made this presentation possible. These divine human beings are:

1) **My Parents**

I was blessed with suitable parentage in the form of Pandit Bisnauth Tiwari (my dad) and Sumintra Bisnauth Tiwari (my mother); my parents lived in the mandir complex at Blairmont Sugar Estate, in the County of Berbice in Guyana, South America.

During the first six (6) years of my life, my dad was the resident priest of the mandir at Blairmont. During this period, I was exposed to worship (Puja), hearing the transcendental glories and pastimes of The Lord (shravanam) and chanting of The Lord's names (kirthanam).

2) **My Mousa (uncle) and Mousee (aunt)**

I lived with my mousa (uncle) and mousee (aunt) from the ages of six (6) to twelve (12). Worship (puja) was done twice daily in their home. Weekends were spent accompanying my Mousa (uncle) on his priestly (pandit) assignments; thus, my exposure to spiritual life which begun in the home of my parents, were consolidated in my mousa (uncle) and mousee's (aunt) home.

3) Bharat Seva Ashram Sangha

During my teenage years, Bharat Seva Ashram Sangha (an association devoted to the promotion of our religion) was very popular. Some of its members were very influential in promoting my spiritual growth: these devotees were Cha Cha (uncle) Seeraj, Cha Cha (uncle) Boodhoo, Mamu Mahadeo Singh (my mother's brother), Cha Cha (uncle) Lambert, Cha Cha (uncle) Baab Chookoon, Nowrang Dada (brother) and my eldest brother Harman.

4) Earl John

I met Earl John in 1962 at a time when I was in a very dark place; I was in a cul-de-sac filled with difficulties and I was lacking the mental maturity to see my way out of them.

Though it was not the done thing to be seen and be associated with me, Earl, who was personnel manager of Blairmont Sugar Estate (the place of my birth and abode), singled me out for empathic attention. He mentored and aided me in the art of converting breakdowns into breakthroughs. He actively encouraged me to carve a career in education and to continue my spiritual pursuits.

He used his influence to gain me employment as a teacher in a local primary school and created the conditions for me to come to the UK in 1968, to pursue a future in education.

5) Chetram Singh

Mr Chetram Singh was the chairman of a panel of interviewers responsible for determining my suitability to pursue further study in the UK. Apart from Mr Singh, the other panellists' line of questioning, were aggressive and hostile which unsettled me. Mr Singh recognized my discomfort and made me feel at ease. He was empathic and constructive. I left the interview thinking that my application was unsuccessful. To my surprise, my application was successful. Years later, I was to learn that he was able to persuade his colleagues that I was worthy of support.

6) Tarawattee Devi

My wife Tarawattee Devi came into my life at a time when I was extremely mentally immature. She brought stability into my life, supported me in my quest to carve a career in education, structured our home so that it was compatible with the pursuit of education, and spiritual growth. She actively collaborated with our children Radha Devi and Vijay Vishnu.in encouraging and supporting me, in my pilgrimage (Yatras) trips to India.

7) Alvin Kallicharran

I am indebted to my fellow countryman Alvin Kallicharran (former West Indies cricket captain), for sharing his religious experiences of India with me. He was gracious in lending me his religious books and invited me to numerous Satsanghas (association of spiritual aspirants) in the Birmingham area.

8) Kishore Lal Balu

Kishore Lal Balu, of Punjabi descent who lives in Birmingham and a very dear friend of mine took me twice to India in 1992, at his own expense. These two trips promoted an intense longing to learn more about our religion. On these trips, I was able to visit Hardwar and Rishikesh (two of the major places of pilgrimage in our religion) which had a spiritually profound effect on me.

9) Sri Krishna and Kanta Bhardwaj

Sri Krishna and his dear wife Kanta who I refer to as Cha Cha (uncle) and Cha Chee (aunt), welcomed me into their home after I delivered a present from his brother to him (Cha Cha).

In his capacity, as Assistant Director General of Telecommunication in India, Cha Cha (uncle) made it possible for me to go on pilgrimages (Yatras), sample life in hermitages (ashrams) as well as being able to access our religious books.

They accompanied me on some of pilgrimages (Yatras) and added to the fund of my knowledge by sharing their experiences of previous visits with me. This was very invaluable. Without their help, I would have remained a spiritual pauper.

10) <u>Sri Virender and Uma Sharma</u>

I was introduced to Sri Virender and his dear wife Uma, the very first time that Sri Krishna (Cha Cha) and his dear wife Kanta (Cha Chee) hosted me in their home. Both Uma and Kanta (Cha Chee) are sisters.

Each subsequent trip to India led to the strengthening of our bond of affection. I refer to Sri Virender as my soul brother (Aatma bhai).

Having retired, Sri Krishna (Cha Cha) and Kanta (Cha Chee) relocated to Gurgaon, which is about two hours' drive from New Delhi. Sri Virender and his dear wife Uma not only hosted me but utilised their network of associates to ensure that each trip to India was spiritually fruitful.

<u>Additional Acknowledgements</u>

I humbly pay tribute to the following persons for their contributions in the preparation of this manuscript.

Nowrang Persaud Dada

I am very grateful to Nowrang Dada for sharing his ideas with me, pointing me in the right direction and for his continued encouragement, throughout the preparation of this manuscript.

ii) Sue Luteman

This manuscript has reached the stage of publication, because Sue willingly utilised her computing skills to aid its typing including, the insertion of religious symbols and initial design of the cover. Her patience, approachability and willingness to help aided in the progress of this manuscript.

iii) Devindra Ramdehal

The final version of the cover is the brainchild of Devindra, who has drawn on his experience of the world of marketing, publishing and Hinduism (Sanatan Dharma) in North America in its design.

iv) Vijay Vishnu Bisnauth

Vijay Vishnu, has brought to bear his skills of computing, experience and expertise of the world of publishing, to provide guidance and motivation throughout the preparation of this manuscript.

The Author

The author is a retired Senior Lecturer (Birmingham City University) whose abiding desire has always been to be a knowledge-based practitioner of Hinduism (Sanatan Dharma).

In spite of the fact that I hail from an orthodox family of Hindu (Sanatanist) priests, from Blairmont Sugar Estate (in the County of Berbice in Guyana), my quest to learn about our religion did not yield anything. Most devout practitioners had access only to a Tulsi Ramayan and a small copy of the Bhagavadgita.

In 1992 I had the opportunity to visit India and during this trip, I met Shri Krishna Bhardwaj, now retired Assistant General of Telecommunications in India, whose help made it possible over the ensuing years for me to go on pilgrimage to Badrinath, Kedarnath, Gangotri, Yamunotri, Rishikesh, Hardwar, Kurukshetra, Vridavan, Mathura, Ayodha, Varanasi, Prayag, Gaya, Rameshwaram and Dwarka.

I was able to sample life in Ashrams at Gangotri, Rishikesh, Hardwar, Prayag and New Delhi. Over the years of visiting India, I was able to access and purchase numerous books on Hinduism (Sanatana Dharma).

A combination of Pilgrimage trips, time spent in Ashrams and access to religious books, have greatly expanded my fund of knowledge of our religion and this book is the end product, which I whole heartedly share with all those who are as keen as I am, to be a knowledge-based practitioner.

Contents

1

Hinduism (Sanatan Dharma) in General

Origin of the word Hindu

Knapp (2008) in an article **about the name Hindu** stated, that most scholars concluded, that the word **Hindu** came into existence, because invaders had difficulties pronouncing the name of the **River Sindhu** properly.

He goes on to add, that some sources of information indicated, that **Alexander the Great**, omitted the the letters **S** and **H** from the word **Sindhu** thus, **Sindhu** became **Indu.** As it was easy to pronounce.

Knapp (2008) goes on to affirm that when invaders from Afghanistan and Persia came to India, they named the **Sindhu River** as **Hindu** and referred to the inhabitants of the **Northwest Province** where the **Sindhu River** was located as **Hindus.**

Knapp's (2008) account of the word **Hindu** is supported by Arjun (1983), Swami Purnananda (1956) and Swami Vivekananda (2001).

There is no religion called Hinduism

Nityananda (1996) sees **Hinduism** as a way of life, rather than as a religion. He goes on to state that the words

Hindu and **Hinduism** are of foreign rather than of Indian origin. He further added that **Hinduism** is a wrong popular name, ascribed to **Sanatan Dharma**- the most ancient and mother of all religions.

What is Sanatan Dharma?

Sanatan - Eternal

Dharma - Virtuous conduct

What is virtuous conduct?

Virtuous conduct is doing what is right, according the order of The Ishwar (The Lord), as laid down in the shastras (religious books and which is reinforced in each avatar(descent) of Ishwar (The Lord) into the material world.

Why our religion is called Sanatan Dharma?

Our religion is referred to as Sanatan (eternal) Dharma (virtuous conduct) because it refers to a scheme of eternal truths, which is applicable to both human and celestial beings; this scheme originated from Ishwar (The Lord) who is samagram (absolute) Sat (existence), samagram (absolute) Cit (consciousness/ awareness) and samagram (absolute) Anandam (bliss).

Key Principles of Hinduism (Sanatan Dharma)

i) There is one God

"Ekam (one) Sat (absolute existence) bipra (The Lord)

13

bahuda (many) badanti (they say) "

Translation

Translation

God is one, yet different people call Him by different names.

Aum Hindutvam p25.

ii) This one God is all beings

The following statements confirm that this one God is in all beings thus:

a) Aham (I am) Aatma (the self or soul) sarva (of all) bhuta (living beings) aashya-sthitah (situated in the heart).

Translation

I (The Lord) the self (Aatma) is seated or located in the hearts of all beings.

Gita
2:20

b) Aatma (the self) ansya(its) jantoh (of all beings) nihita (is seated) guhyam (in the cave of the heart).

Translation
The self (Aatma) is seated in the cavity of the heart of all living beings.   Kathopanisad 1:11:20.

14

iii) <u>The self or soul (Aatma) is a fragment of God</u>

Mama (my) eva (only) amsha (fragment or particle) jiva (indivdual) loke (world), jiva bhuta (the living being) sanatana (eternal).

<u>Translation</u>

The living being of this world is an eternal fragment of My Own Self.

Gita 15:7

iv) <u>This human body is the temple of The Lord</u>

This human body (sthula sharira) is the is the temple (mandir)of The Lord (Ishvar)) because, He is in residence as The Lord within (Antaryami). Gita 10:20 is supportive of the above statement in the following manner:

Aham (I am) Aatma (the self or soul) sarva (of all) bhoota (living beings) aashayah-sthitah (located within the heart).

<u>Translation</u>

I am The Self or Soul of all living beings and I am located in the heart

<u>Additional translation</u>

Since this body is the temple of The Lord, it should be treated with sanctity and purity.

15

v) There should be no enmity towards anyone

Since the Self or The Lord (Aatma or Paramatma), is in all (sarva) beings(bhutesu) and we are all His eternal fragments (amsha), there should be no enmity (nirvairah) or ill will, towards our brothers and sisters of His creation (srsti).

vi) This body is impermanent

This body (sharira) came from the world, it belongs to the world and it will return to the world at death. It came from food, it is eaten by food and it will return to food.

vii) Role of this body

The Lord (Aatman or Paramatman) has given us this human birth, so that we can utilise it, as a vehicle to gain freedom from limitations (moksha). This human body has three names. These are:

a) Mandir (temple)

This human body (ksetram) is a temple (mandir) because The Lord (Paramatma or Aatma), is in residence as The Lord (the antaryami) located in the heart.

As long as the self or soul (Paramatma or Aatma) is in residence, this human body (ksetram) is alive; once The Lord (Paramatma or Aatma has departed from it, it becomes lifeless and death is said to have occurred.

b) <u>Sharira</u>

This body is also called sharira which means, that which is liable to decay.

c) <u>Deha</u>

It is named as deha or that which is to be burnt.

Hinduism (Sanatan Dharma) is a Religion of Universal Love

Hinduism (Sanatan Dharma) is a religion of universal love, care, concern and empathy for all members of God's creation. Some examples which amplifies this are:

1) The Gayatri Mantra

Om bhur bhuva svah, Om tat savitur varenyam, Om bhargo devasya dheemahi, Om dhiyo yo na prachodayat, Om.

Om (the protector) bhur (basis of life) bhuvah (whose contact frees the soul) svah (who pervades and sustains the whole world)

Om (the protector) Tat (That Transcendental Lord) savitur (creator and energiser) varenyam (who is fit to be adored)

Om (the protector) bhargo (who make us pure) devasya (giver of happiness) dheemahi (let us embrace and meditate on Him)

Om (the protector) dhiyo (intellect and understanding) yo na (may our God) pracho dayat (direct, enlighten and guide)

Om (the protector)

Translation

We pray to God who is our protector, the basis of our lives, whose contact frees the soul from the bondage of birth and death and who pervades and sustains the whole world; may this transcendental Lord, who is the creator and energiser of the whole world, who is fit to be adored, make us pure and happy. May He guide and enlighten our intellect in the right direction.

Japa Yoga p 59-67; Prayer Guide
130-13

ii) Peace Invocation

Om Saha nau avatu, Saha nau bhunaktu, Saha viryam karavavaahai, Tejasvi nau adhiitam astu, Maa vidvisaah vahai. Om shanti, Om shanti Om shanti.

OM (the protector) saha (together) nau (both of us) avatu (let Him protect) saha (together) nau (both of us) bhunaktu (come to enjoy the bliss of knowledge)
saha (together) viryam (effort) karava vahai (let us both do)
tejasvi (well studied) nau (both of us) adhitam astu (what we studied) ma (never) vidvisa vahai (quarrel with each other)
OM (the protector) Shanti (save us from all harm emanating from the the sky eg thunder, lightening-and the demigods -adhidaivika)

OM (the protector) Shanti (save us from all harm coming from this earth including, everyone and everything associated with it - adhibhautika)
OM (the protector) Shanti (save us from self harm – (adhiyatmika).

Translation of Peace Invocation
May the Lord protect and nourish us with knowledge, so that what we study, makes sense to us; may we not quarrel or have misunderstanding with each other. May we have peace and protection, from forces over which we have no control i.e, thunder, lightning and the demigods (adhidaivika). May we have peace and protection from all harm, emanating from this world including everyone and everything associated with it (adhibhautica) May we have peace within ourselves so that, we are free from fears, anxieties, and doubts (adhiyatmica).

References
Swami Chinmayananda (2000)-Katha Upanisad (A dialogue with death)-CCMT, Mumbai 400 072, India- 1:1:20 Peace Invocation.

Knapp S (2008) - About The http://www.stephen.knapp.com/

Swami Lokeswarananda (2009)-Katha Upnisad-Ramakrishna Mission of Culture, Kolkatta, 700 029, India-1:1:20& Invocation.

Nath P.V (2002)-Tat Tvam Asi (The Universal Message in The Bhagavadgita)-Motilal Banarsidas, Delhi, 110 007, India-2:20&15:7.

Swami Nityananda (1996)-Symbolism in Hinduism-CCMT, Mumbai, 400 072, India-Page 10.

Swami Prabhupada (1985)-The Bhagavad Gita (As it is)-Bhaktivedanta Book Trust, Watford, Herts, WD2 4XA, UK-12:20 & 15:7.

Swami Purnanda (1956)- Aum Hindutvam- Swami Purnanda, London, W12, UK- Page 25.

Swami Ramsukhdas (2005)- Bhagavadgita (Sadhaka Sanjivini)-Gita Press, Gorakhpur, 273005, UP, India-2:20 &15:7.

Swami Dayananda Saraswati (2005) - Prayer Guide-Arsha Vidya Gurukulum, Pennsylvania, USA- Page 130-132.

Swami Dayananda Saraswati (2006)-Bhagavad Gita (Home Study Course)- Arsha Vidya Gurukulum, Coimbatore, 641 108, India-2:20 & 15:7.

Swami Sivananda (1967)- Japa Yoga-Divine Life Society, Tehri Garhwal, UP, India-Page59-67.

A Resume of books on Hinduism Sanatan Dharma)

There are six (6) categories of books in Hinduism (Sanatan Dharma), these are:

1) Shrutis - that which has been heard and are of Divine origin.

2) Smritis - that which is to be remembered.

3) Itihasa - gives coverage to parables and stories, which are designed, to re- inforce the principles of the Vedas (knowledge) and laws of the Smritis (that which is to be remembered).

4) Puranas - convey the message of the Vedas, in an easy to understand style, in order to educate the masses.

5) Agamas - deals with the worship of a particular aspect of God.

6) Darshanas - are schools of philosophy based on the Shruti (that which has been heard).

A brief account of each book, will now be given.

1 The Shrutis

Definition of Shrutis

That which has been heard, revealed or received intuitively and are of Divine origin. It is a treasure house of knowledge thus, it is called the book of wisdom.

Who were recipients of this revelation?

Great Rsis (saints) who performed austerities (tapasya), and which were pleasing to The Lord, were deemed worthy, to receive the Shrutis (that which has been heard).

The Shrutis (that which has been heard) are referred to as:- The Vedas

Definition of Vedas

Vedas are knowledge of God which have existed throughout time. They are of Divine origin (apauruseya).

Parents of the Vedas

Lord Vishnu is the source of the Vedas, as they originated from the vibration of His vocal chords (OM); thus, Lord Vishnu is their father and Gayatri Mata (mother) is their mother.

Vedas and creation

Knowledge of the Vedas were revealed to the creator of the universe (Brahma)) by Lord of the world (Vishnu); these revelations constitute the authority of The Lord

Number of Vedas

There are four (4) Vedas. These are:

1) **Rg Veda.**

2) **Yajur Veda.**

3) **Sama Veda.**

4) **Atharva Veda.**

Each Veda will now be commented on briefly:

1) Rg Veda

Definition of Rg Veda

The word Veda originated from **"Vid** "the Sanskrit root **"to know "**. In it are to be found Divine and philosophical knowledge.

Age of Rg Veda

It is the oldest of the Vedas and, it is the oldest book in Sankrit or any Indo-European language. It is dated before 4000 B.C. by modern western scholars.

Its coverage includes

- Ancient prayers for victory, wealth, health, longevity and off springs.
- Accounts of origin of the world.
- Politics, economics, social and religious aspects of Vedic civilization.
- Hints of the path to be followed for one's self upliftment.

Upanisad (spiritual/sacred wisdom) found in the Rg Veda

- Aitareya Upanisad is part of the Rg Veda.

2) Yajur Veda

Definition of Yajur Veda

Yajus refers to **"prose mantra** "and Veda denotes **"knowledge".**

Age of Yajur Veda

It is estimated to be in the region of 1200 to 1000 B. C.

Its coverage includes

- Hymns used in religious rituals.
- Moksha or liberation.
- Leadership and power.
- Bravery and fame.

Division of Yajur Veda

i) Krishna (black) Yajur Veda.

The above term refers to an unclear and not wel- organized collection of verses.

ii) Shukla (white) Yajur Veda

Upnisads found in Yajur Veda are:

- Brhadaranyaka
- Isha
- Taittirya
- Katha
- Shwetashvatara
- Maitri

3) Sama Veda

Definition of Sama Veda

Sama comes from the word **"saman or melody"** and Veda pertains to **"knowledge"**. It is a collection of hymns which are meant to be sung.

Its coverage includes

- A collection of hymns in praise of The Lord.
- It is the Veda of devotion (bhakti)
- It represents the force of spiritual knowledge.
- 95% of it contents originated from Rg Veda.
- Sports, art and literature

Upanisads found in Sama Veda are

- Chandogya

- Kena

4) Atharva Veda

Definition of Atharva Veda

It is the storehouse of knowledge for everyday life (atharvanas)

Its coverage includes

- Rituals
- Magic spells
- Wealth
- Primary source of information about Vedic life

Upanisads found in Atharva Veda are:

- Mandukya
- Manduka
- Prashna

Number of Sub Vedas (Upavedas)

There are four (4) Sub Vedas (Upavedas), these are:

1. Ayurveda - composed by Rishi (a purified person) Dhanwantari. Its coverage includes health promotion and maintenance
2. Dhanur Veda - authored by Rishi (a purified person) Vishvamitra, it houses information about weapons and archery.
3. Ghandarva Veda- is about art and music and is composed by Narada Muni.

4. Sthapatya Veda - deals with arts and crafts.

Six Limbs of The Vedas are:

1. Shiksha (phonetics) covers speech, sounds and their production; It was authored by Sage (saint) Panini.

2. Vyakaarana (Grammar) -refers to rules in language, for changing form of words into sentences. This was written by Sage (saint) Panini.

3. Nirukta (Etymology) -is about the origins and history of words and their meaning.

4. Kalpa (Code of Rituals) -the focal point is on the science of rituals and ceremonies in religious rites.

5. Chandas (Literature) - provides information on sounds, and rhythms in poetry and speech.

6) Jyotisha (Astronomy) - gives coverage to science of the stars, planets and astrology.

Divisions or Classifications of the Vedas

There are three (3) divisions or classification of The Vedas (Divine and philosophical knowledge). These are:

i) Karma Kanda

Defintion of Karma Kanda

Karma - action

Kanda - section

This part gives exposure to the role of action.

Aim of Karma (action) Kanda (section)

The aim of action (karma) is to provide selfless service (niskama karma) as a labour of love, so that the mind (antah-karana) gains purity (shuddhi) in order for it to become receptive to the fact that **each individual is The Self/Soul-Aatma** and, **this Self/Soul (Aatma) and The Lord (Paramatma) are one and the same.**

Actions (karmas) and their outcomes

Within this section (kanda) there are different actions (karmas) (actions) to achieve different outcomes; these are:

i) Actions (karmas) to satisfiy one's desires (kamya)) eg to gain heaven (jyotisttoma), or to gain offsprings (putresyajna).

ii) Daily (nitya) actions (karmas) - these are performed daily depending on one's stage of life (ashrama).

The stages (ashramas) and their roles are:

- Brahmachari (student) - pursuit of academic and spiritual education.

- Grhastha (householder) - caters for the welfare of the family and the wider community.

- Vanaprastha (retired) -practice control of the mind and senses; spend time in contemplation.

- Sannyasa (renunciate) - focus is on seeking to see the Aatma (Self/Soul) and Paramatma (The Lord) as one and the same and seeing unity in diversity.

iii) Actions (karmas) that which ought to be done (kartavya)

These actions are determined by our:

- Parents
- Teachers
- Employers
- Government.

iv) Purification (samskara) actions (karmas)

Some examples of purificatory (samskara) actions (karmas) are seen at:

- Conception
- Birth
- Before commencement of schooling
- Sacred thread ceremony (janeo)

ii) <u>Upasana Kanda</u>

<u>What is Upasana?</u>

Upa - near

29

Asana - sitting

Kanda - section

Upasana - mentally sitting near the object of our contemplation, so that we can imbibe the qualities of the contemplated into our daily lives.

Some examples of Upasana (contemplation/worship) are:

- Vishnu (Lord of The World)

- Rama (The 7th incarnation of Vishnu)

- Krishna (The 8th incarnation of Vishnu)

- Shiva (An expression of Vishnu)

- Ganesh (An expression of Vishnu)

Aim of Upasana (contemplation/worship)

The aim of contemplation/worship (upasana) is to gain purity of the mind (antah-karana shuddhi) so that, it is receptive to knowledge (vidya), that **each living being is the Self/Soul (Aatma) and this Self/Soul (Aatma) and The Supreme Lord (Paramatma) are one and the same.**

iii) Jnana Kand

What is Jnana?

Knowledge (jnana) is the agency which removes our ignorance (avidya) that we are the body-mind-complex (ksetram); it reminds us that we **are The Self/Soul (Aatma) and That this Self /Soul (Aatma) and The Lord (Paramatma) are one and the same.**

Aim of Jnana

The aim of knowledge (jnana) is to remind the spiritual aspirant (sadhaka) that **there is no difference between The Self/Soul (Aatma) and The Lord (Paramatma).** This knowledge (vidya) is referred to as self knowledge. (Aatma vidya).

Knowledge (jnana) section (kanda) is referred to as

Ved (Vedas) anta (end portion) or Upanisad.

Definition of Upanisad

According to Swami Dayananda Saraswati (2006), it deals with vidya (knowledge) of Brahman (The Lord); in order to acquire this vidya (knowledge), Swami Tejomayananda (1995) states that the sadhaka (spiritual aspirant), with reverence, respect, and a burning desire, should approach an acharya (spiritual master), sit at his feet and focus his antah-karana (mind) on his master's teaching.

Number of Upanisads

1. 280 Upanisads have been discovered.

2. 108 of the 280 Upanisads are deemed as genuine.

Ten (10) of the Upanisads are well known

These are:

1. Aitareya (from Rg Veda)

31

2. Katha and Taittiriya (from Krishna Yajur Veda)

3 Brhadaranyaka and Ishavasya (from sukla Yajur Veda)

4 Kena and Chandogya (from Sama Veda)

5 Mundaka, Mandukya and Prashna (from Atharva Veda)

Swami Dayananda Saraswati 2006

2) Smritis

Definition of Smritis

The Smritis (that which is remembered) are the second of the listed books in Hinduism (Sanatan Dharma); They are a manual of social, ethical and moral conduct.

Origin of the Smritis

The Vedas or Srutis (that which has been revealed) are apauraseya (of transcendental origin) and were revealed to Rishis (purified devotees). These Rishis (purified) persons committed these Divine revelations to memory; they then spread the Smritis (memorised message) to society per se.

Number of Smritis

There are eighteen (18) Smritis.

Role of the Smritis

The Smritis provide guidance to us humans, on how to maximise our lives in a moral and ethical manner. They provide codes and rules governing actions of individuals, local community, and society at large and nations. These codes and rules constitutes **Laws governing right conduct (Dharma Shastras).** The most important Dharma Shastra (laws governing right conduct) is the Manu Smriti

3) Itihasa

Definition of Itihasa

Itihasa is the Sanskrit word for history and refers to narrations, which occurred during the lifetime of the narrator. It is the third set of books in Hinduism (Sanatan Dharma).

Format of the Itihasa

The Itihasa is in the form of stories and parables which are designed, to reinforce the principles of the Vedas and Smritis in this age we live in.

The most important Itihasa are:

a) The Ramayana

What is the Ramayana?

It is the epic story of Sri Rama (the 7th incarnation Vishnu - The Lord of the world.)

What was the objective Sri Rama's incarnation?

The objective of this incarnation was to re-establish:

- Satya (the religion of truth).

- Dharma (virtuous conduct).

Who were the principal actors in the Ramayan?

The principal actors were:

i) Sri Rama - (representing Knowledge - jnana)

ii) His consort Sri Sita Ji - (representing devotion - bhakti)

iii) Lakshman - his brother (representing Vairagya - dispassion and tapas – austerity)

iv) Bharata - His brother (who was an embodiment of selfless love for the Lord)

v) Satrughana - His brother (who was an embodiment of selfless service for the Lord)

vi) Hanuman - His devotee (who was an embodiment of loyalty and devotion in the service of the. Lord).

Seven sections of the Ramayan are:

i)   Bala Kanda - Sri Rama's childhood.

ii) Ayodha Kanda -Sri Rama's life in Ayodha before his exile.

iii) Aranya Kanda - His life in the forest and abduction of his consort Sri Sita Ji by Ravana.

iv) Kishkinda Kanda - Sri Rama's stay with his monkey ally in his capital.

v) Sundara Kanda - Sri Rama's journey to Sri Lanka.

vi) Yuddha (Lanka) Kanda - his successful battle against Ravana and recovery of His spouse Sri Sita Ji.

vii) Uttara kanda - His life as king of Ayodha.

b) The Mahabharata

Definition of Mahabharata

Maha - great

Bharata - Bharata

Mahabharata - Great tale of the Bharat dynasty.

Mahabharata is a Sanskrit epic, which was concerned with the dynastic struggle and civil war, for the throne of Hastinapur, contested by the kauravas brothers headed by Duryodhana (the forces of evil) and the pandava brothers led by Yudhistira (the forces of righteousness). This war was fought at Kurukshetra in northern India in the 9th century B. C. The Mahabharata is the world's largest epic in existence with 100,000 verses, authored by Vyasa and with Lord Ganesh as the stenographer.

It contains the following information

i) Bhagavad Gita - A discussion between Sri Krishna (the 8th incarnation of Vishnu), on how to overcome conflict and grief in order to experience one's real nature i.e., **The Self/Soul (Aatma)**. Sri Krishna informs us that **The Self/Soul (Aatma) and The Lord (Paramatma) are one and the same.**

ii) It houses every branch of knowledge e.g. science, arts, commerce, economics, politics, warfare, social science, history mythology, and Dharma Shastra (religious duties).

4) The Puranas

What are The Puranas?

They are a collection of stories, hymns, history, rules of living, rituals, and knowledge of the world. They are the fourth (4) set of books in our religion.

Number of Puranas

There are eighteen (18); the most popular are:

- Sri mad Bhagavatam

- Vishnu Purana

- Markandeya Purana

Role of The Puranas
They are meant to preserve the culture of our religion and explain the knowledge of the Vedas in easy to understand style

Areas covered by the Puranas are:

- Sarga (creation).

- Pratisarga (destruction).

- Vamsha (genealogy).

- Manvantara (period of a Manu - universal administrator for religion and virtuous conduct).

- Vamshacharita (history)

5) The Agamas

What are the Agamas?

They are the fifth (5) set of books in Hinduism (Sanatan Dharma); they are Shastras (group of religious books) which provide practical guidance of Divine worship.

Areas of coverage are:

- Study of the universe
- Study of the nature of knowledge
- Meditation
- Construction of mandirs
- Mantras (a form of words to aid spiritual growth), Yantras (a mystical diagram to give protection and aid spiritual growth), and tantras (application of cosmic sciences to aid spiritual growth).
- Worship of God

Divisions of the Agamas are:

i)   Shiva Agama - devoted to worship of Shiva (an   expression of Lord Vishnu).

ii)   Vaishnava Agama -dedicated to the worship of The Lord Vishnu.

iii) Shakti Agama -committed to the praise of Devi (the universal mother).

6) The Darshanas

What are the Darshanas?

The Darshanas are the sixth (6) and last set of books in Hinduism (Sanatan Dharma). The word Darshana means **"vision"**. They refer to schools of philosophy based on the Shrutis (that which has been heard, revealed or received intuitively and are of Divine origin).

Number of Darshanas

There are six (6) Schools of Darshanas, these are:

i) Nyaya School of Darshanas -Deals with logic and reasoning. It was founded by Rishi (saint) Gautama.

ii) Vaiseshika School of Darshanas - talks about the universe being made up of countless atoms. It was authored by Rishi (saint) Kanada.

iii) Yoga School of Darshanas - came into being because of Patanjali to prepare the body and mind to be receptive to Aatma (Self/ Soul) vidya (knowledge) i.e. **we are the Self/Soul (Aatma) and not the body/mind/intellect complex (ksetram).**

iv) Sankhya School of Darshanas - here the Sage (saint) Kapila informs us about Prakrti (nature) and Purusa (Spirit).

v) Purba Mimamsa School of Darshanas -presented by the Sage (saint) Jaimini, focuses on rituals and yajna (sacrifices).

vi) Vedanta School of Darshanas - this school led by the Sage (saint) Badarayana (Vyasa), said that realization of The Supreme Lord is possible by self experience.

References

Swami Chinmayananda (2000)-Aitareya Upanisad (Preface to Revisedd Edition) CCMT, Mumbai, 400 072, India- Page 1.

Swami Dayananda Saraswati (2006)- Mundako Upanisad (An Introduction) Arsha Vidya Centre for Research and Publication, Chennai, 600 004, India-Vol 1 p 6-7.

Swami Tejomayananda (1995)- Hindu Culture (An Introduction)-CCMT, Mumbai, 400 072, India- p 41-43.

Bibliographies

Arjun H (1983) - Hindu Dharma (Devotional Prayers and Rites)-Sharada Press, Mangalore 571 001. India.

Jairam B (1993) - Goldenn Teachings of Hinduism (Dharmik Prakash)-Dharmik Books, W.H. Inc, Canada.

Jagannathan (1994)-Hinduism (An Introduction)-Vakils, Feffer and Simons Ltd, Bombay, India.

Swami Jagdishwarananda (1977) - Sanatan Dharma (A Key to understanding Hindu Religion) - Publisher Unknown.

Swami Nityananda (1996) Symbolism in Hinduism - C. C. M. T, Mumbai, 400 072, India.

Swami Purnanda (1980) Aum Hindutvam (Vedic Prayer and Hindu Catechism)- Swami Purnananda, London, W12, UK

Sarma D (1981) - A Primer of Hinduism - Sri Ramakrishna Math, Mylapore, Madras, 600 004, India.

Swami Swahananda (Unknown)-Hindu Symbology and other essays-Sri Ramakrish Math, Mylapore, Chennai, 600 004, India.

Swami Tejomayananda (1955) -Hindu Culture (An Introduction)-CCMT, Mumbai, 400 072, India.

Swami Vivekananda (2001) - Essentials of Hinduism - Advaita Ashram, Mayawati, Himalayas, India.

Swami Nikhlananda (1947) Aatma Bodha of Sri Shankaracarya-Madras, 600 004, India.

3

God in Hinduism (Sanatan Dharma

There is only one God in Hinduism (Sanatan Dharma)

Non-Hindus (non Sanatanists) and those who label themselves as Hindus (Sanatanists), believe that Hinduism (Sanatan Dharma) is a religion of many Gods; this belief or opinion is grossly inaccurate as there is only one God in our religion.

The following statements give support to the fact, that there is only one God in Hinduism (Sanatan Dharma):

i)Ekam Sat bipra bahudha badanti

 Ekam(one) Sat (absolute existence) bipra (The Lord) bahuda (may) badanti (they say).

Translation

God is one, yet different people call Him by different names.

Rg Veda cited in Hindutvam, p25

ii) Aatma- mayam samaavisya, so aham gunamayim dvija; srajan raksan haran vishvam, dadhre samjnaa kriyocitam

Aatma mayam (my energy) samvishaya (having entered) so ham (myself), gunamayim (composed of modes of material nature) dvija (O twice born);

Srjan (creating) saksan (maintaining) haran (annihilating) visvam (the cosmic manifestation), dadhre (I cause to be born) sanjnyam (a name) kriyochitam (according to the activity).

Translation

My dear Vidura, reflecting in my universal power (maya), composed of the modes of material nature (gunas), I create, sustain, and annihilate this universe; I assume three different names according to the acts I perform.

Shrimad Bhagvatam 4:7:51

iii) When the Lord creates, He is called Brahma, when He sustains, He is referred to as Vishnu; When He dissolves creation, He assumes the name of Shiva.

Mundakopanisad vol 1, p 26-27

iv) Avibhaktam ca bhutesu, vibhaktam iva ca sthitam; bhuta-bhartr ca taj jneyam, grasisnu prabhavisnu ca.

Avibhaktam (without division) ca (also) bhutesu (in all living beings), vibhaktam (divided) iva (as if) ca (and) sthitam (remaining);

bhuta bhatr (the sustainer of all living beings) ca (also) tat (that) jneyam (to be known), grasisnu (the devourer) prabha vishnu (the creator) ca (and)

Translation

He (The Lord) seems to be distributed amongst all living beings: but in reality, He (The Lord) is never divided rather, He (The Lord) is situated as one; He who is the creator, sustainer and the devourer of all creation, is the only one worth knowing.

Gita:13:17

v) Yah (He the great Lord) ekah (one without a second)

Translation

The Lord is one without a second.

Shetashvatara Upanisad
4;1

vi) There is only one single reality in this world, and that reality appears to be many, because of different names and forms superimposed on it.

Chandogya Upanisad 6:1:4:
p484.

vii) Eko vasi sarva bhuta -antarAatma

Antar (the innermost) Aatma (self or soul) sarva (of all) bhuta (beings) ekah (is one and the same) vashi (ruler and controller of all).

<u>Translation</u>

The innermost self of all beings, is one and the same and is the ruler and controller of all.

Kathopanisad 2:5:12:
P223

Kathopanisad 2:2:11:
p151

This one God is eternal

Aksaram (indestructible) Brahma (The lord) Param (Limitless) svabahva (eternal nature) adhytam (that which is centred on the body) ucyate (is called).

<u>Translation</u>

The Supreme Lord is limitless, indestructible and not subject to change. Its manifestation in the body is called Jiva (the embodied living).

This one God is supreme and perfect

The following mantras emphasizes this point very well.

i) Om purnam adah purnam idam, purnaat purnam udacyate; purnasya purnam aadaaya, purnam eva avashisyate

Om (the complete whole) purnam (perfectly complete) adah (That) purnam (perfectly complete) idam (this phenomenal world), purnat (from the all perfect) purnam (complete unit) udacyate (is produced);

purnasya (of the complete whole) purnam (completely all) adaya (having been taken away), purnam (the complete balance) eva (even) avshisyate (is remaining).

Translation

The supreme Lord is perfect and complete thus, because He is perfectly complete, all emanations from Him including this world and creation are complete wholes; any product of the complete whole is also complete-in it self.

Ishopanisad Invocation

ii) Om isha idam sarvam yat - kinca jagatyam jagat; tena tyktena bhunjitha, ma grdhah kasya svid dhanam.

Isha (by The Lord) avasyam (controlled) idam (this) sarvam (all) yat kinca (whatever) jagatyam (within the world) jagat (changing world),

tena (by Him) tyktena (by renunciation) bhunjitah (you should enjoy) ma (do not) grdhah (seek to profit) kasya svit (of anyone else) dhanam (wealth).

Translation

Everything in this changing world is owned and controlled by The Lord; one should enjoy what is set aside for him/her and not seek, to profit from the wealth of others. By the process of renunciation, one should seek to experience the self (Aatma) which is within.

Isha upanisad Mantra 1

46

What this one God is

This one God is:

i) Nityam - eternal and immortal thus, it is not bound by time therefore, it is without beginning and end.

ii) Vibhum - it is extensive and full of manifestation thus, it becomes many in the form of the cosmos and changeless.

iii) Sarva gatam - it is all pervading like space. It has no location and is the upadana (the material) karana (cause) as well as nimittika (the efficient) karana (cause) of everything.

iv) Susuksam - It is subtlest of the subtle therefore, it is not available for objectification.

v) Tat avyayam - The Lord is free from decline and disappearance in short, it is imperishable.

Mundakopanisad 1:1:6

Aatman or Brahman (The Self/ Soul)

What is Aatman or Brahaman (The Self/Soul)?

i) Chandogya Upanisad 6:10:3 explains the Aatman or Brahman (the Self/Soul) in the following manner:

Sah yah esah anima idam sarvam, aitadaatmyam, tat satyam sah Aatma tat tvam asi

Sah yah (that which) esah (this) anima (the subtlest of all), idam (this) sarvam (of all) aitadaatmyam (the Self) tat (that) satyam (The absolute Truth);
Sah (that is) Aatma (the Self) Tat (That) tvam (thou/you) asi (are).

Translation

That which is the subtlest of all, is The Self of all this. This is the absolute truth. It is The Self and you are The Self.

ii) The Aatman (Self/Soul) and Brahman (The Lord) are one and the same and is Sat, Cit, Ananda.

What is Sat?

Sat is that which existed in the past, exists now and will exist in the future thus, it is present in all three periods of time. It is:

- Anadi (beginning less)

- Ajanma (birthless)

- Amara (deathless)

- Ananta (infinite)

- Nitya (timeless)

- Avikari (changeless)

48

- Anami (nameless)

- Nirakara (formless)

- Nirguna (attributeless).

What is Cit?

Cit or consciousness is of the nature of absolute knowledge/awareness. It is present in all three states of experiences eg:

- Jagrata (waking) avastha (state)

- Svapna (dream) avastha (state)

- Susupti (deep sleep) avastha (state)

Cit is also present in the three periods of time:

- Past

- Present

- Future

Ananda or bliss is the very nature of the Aatman (Self /Soul). Aatman (the Self/Soul) Brahman (The Lord) are one and the same.

Taittiriya Upanisad 2:1:1

The Lord was present before creation

Srimad Bhagvatam 2:9:33 reveals that The Lord was present before creation thus:

Aham eva asam eva agre, na anyat yat sat asat param; pashcat aham yate tat ca, yah avashisyeta sah asmi aham

Aham (I-The Supreme Lord) eva (certainly) asam (existed) agre (before creation) na (never) anyat (anything else) yat (all these) sat (the effect) asat (the cause) param (The Supreme);
paschat (at the end) aham (The Supreme Lord) yat (all these) etat (creation) ca (and) yah (everyrthing) avashisyeta (remains) sah (that) asmi (I am) aham (I-The Lord).

Translation

I, The Supreme Lord certainly existed before creation, when there was nothing but itself (The Lord). Material nature, the cause of creation was not there. I, The Supreme Lord is what you see now and at the end of creation, what remains, will be I The Supreme Lord.

The Lord is responsible for creation

The following statements reveal that The Lord is responsible for creation:

i) Maya adhyaksena prakrtih, suyate sa cara-acaram; hetuna anena kaunteya, jagat viparivartate

Maya (by my own) adhyaksena (supervision) prakrtih (the cause of the world), Sooyate (creates) sa (both) caracaram (the world of moving and non-moving); hetuna (for the reason) anena (because) kaunteya (O son of Kunti), Jagat (the world) viparivartate (is functioning)

Translation

Under my supervision, prakrti creates the world of the moving and non-moving beings. For this reason, the world undergoes change.

Gita 9:10

ii) Aham adih ca madhyam ca, bhutanam antah eva ca.

Aham (I) adih (the cause of creation) ca (and) madhyam (middle as well as sustenance) ca (and), bhutanam (of all living beings) antah (end or resolution) eva (also) ca (and).

Translation
I am the cause of creation, its sustenance and its end or resolution.

Gita 10:20

iii) Aatma -mayam samaavisya, sah aham guna-mayim dvija srjan raksan vishvam,

Aatma-mayam (my energy) samaavishya (having entered),
sah (myself) aham ((I) guna-mayim (composed of the modes of material nature) dvija (O twice born);

51

srjan (creating) raksan (maintaining) haran (annihilating) vishvam (the cosmic manifestation)

<u>Translation</u>

O twice born Vidura, reflecting in my maya composed of the three gunas (sattva - mode of goodness, rajas- mode of passion and activity, and tamas-mode of dullness), I create this universe, maintain it and I annihilate it.

Srimad Bhagavatam 4:7:51

iv) Yat ca api sarva bhutanam, bijam tat aham arjuna; na tat asti vinaa yat syaan, maya bhutanam cara-acaram.

Yat (whatever) ca (also) api (maybe) sarva (all) bhutanam (beings/things), bijam (seed/cause) tat (that) aham (I) arjuna (O Arjuna);
na (not) tat (that) asti (there is) vina (without) yat (which) syaan (exists), maya (Me) bhootam (created being) cara (moving) acaram (non-moving)

<u>Translation</u>

O Arjuna, I am the generating seed i.e, the efficient as well as the material cause, of all living beings. There is no creature moving and non-moving that can exist without me. He (The Lord) is the creator as well as the creation.

Gita 10:39

The following statement indicates that the lord is within each one of us:

Mundakopanisad 2:2:7 indicates that the Aatman or Brahman (The Self/Soul) manifest itself in the buddhi (intellect) as Chaitanya (pure consciousness) thus, buddhi (intellect) is referred to as Brahmapure (the city of The Lord) because, Aatma or Brahman can be recognised here in the form chidambara (awareness) in every thought. He (The Lord) is the witness to all our actions.

How to experience The Lord who is within each one of us

Some means of experiencing The Aatman (Self/soul) or Brahman (The Lord) antaryami (within us) are:

i) Possession of a burning desire to gain this experience.

 Mundakopanisad 3:2:3 supports this statement thus:

Yam eva esah vrnute tena labhya, tasya esah aAatma vivrnute tanum svaam.

Yam (whom) eva (alone) esah (this devotee) vrnute (chooses to experience whole heartedly) tena (by him) labhyah (it is gained),
tasya (to him) esah (this) Aatma (self) svam (itself) tanum (its true nature) vivrnute (reveals).

Translation

The self is gained by the devotee, who chooses to experience it whole heartedly; to this devotee, the self reveals its true nature.

ii) It is gained by prayer - (Shvetashvatara Upanisad 2:3)

Yuktvaaya manasa devaan suvaryato dhiyaa divam, brhat jyoti karisyatah Savita prasuvaati tan

Yuktavya (having united) manasa (withy the mind) devan (the sense organs) suvaryutah (turned towards the self) dhiya (through right knowledge) divam (the luminous), brhat (the great) jyoti (light) karisyatah (lead towards) Savita (The Sun God) prasuvaati (bless) tan (them).

Translation

May the Sun God unite our mind and sense organs, so that they are turned towards the luminous Aatman or Brahman (The Self/Soul), through right knowledge. May He (The Sun God - Savita) bless them.

iii) The Aatman or Brahman The Self/Soul) is known through purity of mind; the following statements highlights this point very well:

 a) This One is recognized through citta shuddhi (purity of mind).

Chandogya Upanisad 8:13:1, p793.

54

b) Manasa eva idam aptavyam Manasa (by the mind) eva (alone) idam (this) aptavyam (is to be realized)

Translation

Only by a purified mind alone can this Self (Aatman or Brahman) be realized.

Katha Upanisad 2:4:11

Katha Upanisad 2:1 :11

iv) The Aatman or Brahman (Self/Soul) can be known by religious discipline eg

- Puja (worship).

- Vrat (fasting)

- Mounam (observing silence).

- Yajna (sacrifice).

- Yama and Niyama (Self restraint).

Chandogya Upanisad 8:5:1

v) Clear knowledge

This can be gained by:

- Sravanam - this is an enquiry to ascertain and discover, the exact meaning of the words of Shruti

(Vedas are called Shruti as they are considered as **Shruta or heard**). It is listening to the exposition by an acharya (competent spiritual master), in a spirit of vichara (enquiry) and with shraddha (complete faith)

- Mananam - is a reflection on what has been heard, as read in the religious books or, as expounded by the spiritual master, in order to gain understanding.

- Nididhyasana - is contemplation on the the message in order to clarify doubts or misunderstandings so that learning can take place.

Pancadashi 1:53

vi) Repetition of the great statement

Our shastras (scriptures) advises us to repeat the mahavakya (great statement) **Aham (I am) Brahmasmi (Brahman).**

Translation

I am Brahman (The Lord). This statement is meant to be repeated, until you come to know that you are Aatma (Self/ Soul) It is to be noted, that Aatma (Self/Soul) and Brahman (The Lord) -are one and the same.

Shvetashvatara Upanisad 4:3:
p 129

How to worship this one God

The Lord God can be worshipped in two ways. These are:

i) Worshipping this one God without form

When this one God is worshipped without form (nirguna upasana), He is called Brahman.

According to Swami Dayananda Saraswati (1997), The word Brahman come s from "**brh**" which is translated as" **The Big** "Swami Harshananda (1995) agrees with Swami Dayananda Saraswati's (1997) definition but goes on to add the word **"Infinite"** after **"Big "**.

Our shastras (religious books shas - to ordain, tras - to protect) inform us, that our ancient Rishis (saints), performed nirguna upasana (worshipped God without form), by chanting Aum (OM) the prayer mantra.

ii) Worshipping this one God with form

Those whose antah-karana (minds)) are ashuddhi (impure) and who place emphasis on aham (I am) dehe (this body) and jagat (this material world), find it very difficult to do nirguna upasana (focus on worshipping a formless God).

These sadhakas (group of spiritual aspirants) find it easy, to focus on saguna upasana (worshipping God with attributes); some examples of worshipping Saguna Brahman (god with attributes) are:

- Shiva- (auspicious).

- Ganesh - (remover of obstacles and Lord of new beginnings).

- Rama- (promoter of Satya -absolute Truth and Dharma - virtuous conduct).

- Krishna - (giver of prema -divine love and shanti - peace).

- Devi - (The Divine Mother).

References

Swami Chinmayananda (1997)-Mundakopanisad -C. C. M. T, Mumbai, 400 072, India-1;16, 2:27, 3:23.

Swami Chinmayananda (1998) - Taittiriya Upanisad- C. C. M. T, Mumbai, 400 072, India- 2:1:1

Swami Chinmayananda (2000) – Kathopanisad (A dialogue with death)- CCMT, Mumbai, 400 072, India-2:5:12 and 2:41.

Swami Harshananda (1995) - A Dictionary of Advaita Vedanta-Ramakrishna Math, Bangalore, 560 019, India.

Swami Lokeswarananda (2005) - Swetashvatara Upanisad- Ramakrishna Mission Institute of Culture, Kolkata, 700 029, India-4:3: p129 and 2:3.

Swami Lokeswarananda (2008) - Mundaka Upanisad-Ramakrishna Mission Institute of Culture, Kolkata, 700 029, India-1:16, 2:27 and 3:23.

Swami Lokeswarananda (2009) - Kathopanisad-Ramakrishna Mission Institute of Culture, Kolkata, 700 029, India-2:2:11: p151 and 2;41.

Swami Lokeswarananda (2010) -Chandogya Upanisad - Ramakrishna Mission Institute of Culture, Kolkata, 700 029, India-6:1:4: p484 and 6:10:03.

Nath P.V. (2002) -Tat Tvam Asi (The Universal Message in The Bhagavadgita) - Motilal Banarsidas, Delhi, 110 007, India-9:10,10:20 and 10:39.

Swami Prabhupada (1985)- The Bhagavadgita (As it is) -
Bhaktivedanta Book Trust, Watford, Herts, WD2 4XA,
UK- 9:10,10:20 and 10:39.

Swami Prabhupada (1992) - Srimad Bhagavatam
Bhaktivedanta Book Trust, Watford, Herts, WD2 4XA,
UK- 4:7:51.

Swami Prabhupada (1993)- Shri Ishopanisad -
Bhaktivedanta Book Trust, Watford, Herts, WD2 4XA,
UK- Invocation Mantra1.

Swami Purnananda (1956) - Aum Hindutvam (Vedic
Prayer and Hindu Catechism)- London W12, UK- Page
25.

Swami Ramsukhdas (2005) - Srimad Bhagvadgita
(Sadhaka Sanjivini) - Gita Press, Gorakhpur, UP, India-
9:10, 10:20 and 10:39.

Swami Dayananda Saraswati (1997) – Vivekacudamani
(Talks on 108 Selected Verses) - Sri Gangadhareshvar
Trust, Rishikesh, UP, 249 201, India- Verse 1.

Swami Dayananda Saraswati (2006)- Bhagavadgita
(Home Study Course) Arsha Vidya Gurukulum, Struti
Seva Trust, Coimbatore, Tamil Nadu, 641108, India-
2:1:3:16

Swami Dayananda Saraswati (2006) - Mundakopanisad -
Arsha Vidya Research and Publication, Chennai, 600
004, India- Vol 1: p 26-27, 1:1:6: 2:2:7 and 3:2:3.

Swami Suddhabodhananda (1994) – Panchdashi (Discovering your innate greatness- Sri Viswesar Trust, Bombay, India- 1:53

4

Symbols in Hinduism (Sanatan Dharma)

There are several symbols in Hinduism (Sanatan Dharma). A resume of some will now be given.

1) AUM (OM)

Definition of AUM (OM)

Pranav (that by which God is praised) or AUM (OM), is the single syllable name of The Supreme Lord thus, it has all the attributes of The Supreme Lord i.e

- Samagram (Absolute) Sat (existence).

- Samagram (Absolute) Chit (knowledge /awareness).

- Samagram (Absolute) Ananda (bliss).

AUM (OM) is the best symbol in Hinduism (Sanatan Dharma)

Aum (OM) is universally accepted as the best symbol of Hinduism (Sanatan Dharma), as it means invoking The Ishvar (The Lord) in a single syllable. It is the most holy sound in Hinduism (Sanatan Dharma), because it originated from the vibration of Ishvar's (The Lord's) vocal chords during expiration.

 Composition of AUM (OM)- it is made up of three letters which are: **AUM.**

A

U

M

Each ritual or prayer commences with AUM (OM) and concludes with AUM (OM)

A detailed account will be covered in the chapter on AUM (OM).

2) Swastika

Definition of Swastika

It is the symbol of auspiciousness. It is believed that the symbol Swastika is a combination of:

- Su - meaning good

- Asasti - meaning to exist

Taken together its meaning is **may good exist or prevail**

Diagrammatic representation of Swastika- which represents pathways to freedom from limitations.

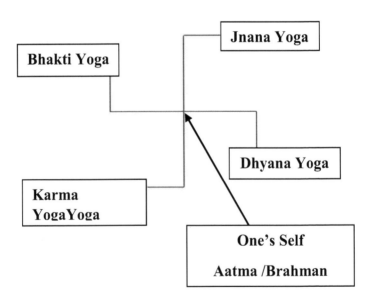

3) The Lotus Flower

The lotus flower symbolizes:

- Antah - karana (mind) Shuddhi (purity of).

- Viveka or discrimination between absolute existence - Sat and impermanent existence -asat.

- Sama (mastery of the mind).

- Dama (mastery of the senses).

- Uparati (detachment in attachment).

- Titiksa (taking the pinpricks of life in its stride without being affected)

- Mumuksutva (a burning desire to be free of its environment)

4) Sankha (Conch shell)

The blowing of the Sankha (conch shell) is a reminder, that we should maximise our allotted lifespan, to experience and to know our real nature which is Aatma or Self/Soul.It is to be noted that Aatma(Self/Soul) and Paramatma (The Lord) are one and the same.

In order to experience our real nature, we need to withdraw the senses from material world and turn within.

5) <u>Chakra</u> (Discus)

The Chakra (Discus) is the wheel of time. It is a reminder that life has a beginning and an end: we are urged to maximise our allotted lifespan, in order to know that we are AAatma (The Self/Soul) and, Aatma (Self/Soul) and ParamAatma (The Lord) are one and the same.

6) <u>Gada</u> (Mace)

It is the symbol that confers antah-karana (the mind) shuddhi (purity).

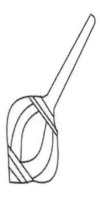

7) <u>Mala</u> (prayer beads)

It is an aid to gain sama (mastery of the mind) and dama (mastery of the senses) so so that both can be productively utilised, to aid spiritual growth.

8) <u>Kamandalu</u> (Water pot)

It symbolizes:

Sannyasa (renunciation) of objects of the senses in favour of experiencing one's real nature i.e. Aatma (Self/Soul). We are reminded that Aatma (Self /Soul) and Paramatma (The Lord) are one and the same.

9) Vehicles

The vehicle of The Creator (Brahma) of the world is Hamsa (the swan).

It represents the ability to see the Ishvar/Paramatama/Brahman (The Lord) everywhere and in everything.

The vehicle of the Vishnu (sustainer of the world) is Garuda (the eagle)

Garuda is a man with and eagle face and wings of a bird. He represents:

- Bhakti (devotion)
- Spiritual and physical strength
- Piety

The vehicle of Shiva (the annihilator) of the world is Nandi (a bull)

Nandi (The bull) represents:

- Ananda (bliss)
- Dharma (virtuous conduct)

Its four legs symbolize:

- Sat (truth)
- Shuddhi (purity)
- Daya (kindness)

- Danam (charity)

The vehicle of Ganesh (Lord of new beginnings) is a mouse

The mouse is the symbol of kama (desires) one of our internal enemies. Riding the mouse indicates He (Ganesh) has conquered kamas (desires)

10) <u>Decorations</u>

Vishnu

- **His blue colour** signifies infinity

- **Yellow garments** symbolize the earth thus, it is said that He is clothed in earth or matter

- **The crown on His head** confirms that He is the sole proprietor of the world.

- **Kaustubha (gem) on His chest** is a symbol of shuddhi (purity), nitya (everlasting) Aatma (The Self/Soul) of jagat (the world).

- **Shesh Nag or Ananta (the serpent) is His bed** and has a thousand heads. The thousand head implies the numerous distractions of the mind. The hoods of Shesha or Ananta are turned inwards indicating that only when the mind is turned within can the Aatma (Self/Soul) be experienced.

- **Lakshmi is the Shakti (power) of Vishnu** (the preserver of or maintainer of the world. Her abode on his chest indicates that wherever He is, She is always present. She provides the resource for maintenance of the world.

Shiva's decoration

Shiva is in charge of constructive destruction; his decorations are:

- **Garland of snakes** seen on his neck. This is symbolic of death and though He is surrounded by it, He is Master of it.

- **His garment is that of a tiger skin** suggesting that He is master of all forces.

- **His matted hair** is a reminder that He is Lord of the Vayu (Air).

- **The crescent moon on His head** is suggestive of His powers of procreation.

- **Ganga is the symbol** of Aatma (The Self/Soul) and vidya (knowledge) i.e, Aham (I am) Brahmasmi (The Lord - Brahman/Paramatma/ Ishvar).

- **His Trishul (Trident)** represents the following:

70

a) He is the Lord of creation, maintenance and constructive destruction,

b) He is the master of the gunas (qualities of the mind)

c) He is the ruler of the past, present and the future.

- **His consort is Parvati** the provider of the power or energy to make constructive destruction possible.

Bibliographies

Braroo A (1994) - Call of the Nine Goddesses -Pustak Sansaar-Jammu180 001, India.

Seth K. N and Chaturvedi B.K(1999) - Gods and Goddesses of India - Diamond Pocket Books Pvt Ltd, New Delhi, 110 006, India.

Swami Nitynanda (1996) - Symbolism in Hinduism - C C M T, Mumbai, 400 072, India.

Swami Swahananda (U) - Hindu Symbology (and other essays)- Sri Ramakrishna Math, Mylapore, Chennai, 600 004, India.

Swami Tejomayananda (1995) - Hindu Culture (An Introduction)- C C M T, Mumbai, 400 072, India.

Swami Harshananda (2000) - Hindu Symbols (Including emblems and sacred Symbols) - Ramakrishna Math, Bangalore, 560 019, India.

5

Importance AUM (OM) in Hinduism (Sanatan Dharma

What is AUM (OM)?

AUM (OM) is defined as follows by the cited references:

i) Kathopanisad 1:2;16 defines AUM (OM) as follows:

Etat hi eva aksaram brahma etat eva hi aksaram param, etat hi eva aksaram jnatva yah yat icchati tasya tat.

Etat (this) hi (verily) eva (that) aksaram (immortal) brahma (The Lord with attributes), Etat (this) hi (eva) aksaram (immortal) param (The Lord without attributes-the highest);
Etat (this) hi (also) eva (that) aksaram (immortal) jnatva (knowing), Yah (whatever) yat (which) icchati (wishes) tasya (to him) tat (that is gained).

Translation

This word AUM (OM) is saguna Brahman (The Lord with attributes). This word AUM (OM) is also nirguna Brahman (The Lord without attributes). The spiritual aspirant who knows this AUM (OM), gains whatever he or she wishes. To know AUM (OM) is to know The Lord.

Taittiriya Upanisad 1:8:1sees AUM (OM) thus:

Om iti brahma, Om iti idam sarvam

AUM (OM) iti (thus) Brahma (The Lord) AUM (OM) Iti (thus) idagm (this world) sarvam (all).

Translation

The word AUM (OM) is Brahman (The Lord) and it represents everything.

Gita 7:8 provide this definition of AUM (OM)

Pranav sarva vedesu

Pranavah (AUM- OM) sarva (in all) vedesu (Vedas)

Translation

I am the word AUM (OM)in all the Vedas.

The origin of AUM (OM)

AUM (OM) is the sound incarnation of Saguna Brahman (the Supreme Lord - with attributes, as it originated from the vibration of His vocal chords, during expiration.

Why rituals/mantras begin and end with AUM (OM)?

AUM (OM) is The Lord and its chanting is done for the following reasons:

- Chanting AUM (OM) before a ritual or mantra, is done, to seek the blessings of The Lord, for a successful outcome.

- Chanting AUM (OM) during the ritual or mantra is to seek The Lord's grace to energize the occasion, so that the sadhaka (spiritual aspirant) is totally immersed in the ritual or chanting to enhance its effectiveness.

- Ending the ritual or mantra with AUM (OM), is necessary because AUM (OM) is The Lord and nothing happens, without His grace.

Taittiriya Upanisad 1:8:1

Composition of AUM (OM)

OM is made up of three (3) letters. These are:

i) **A**

ii) **U**

iii) **M**

Symbolism in Hinduism (Sanatan (Dharma) p71

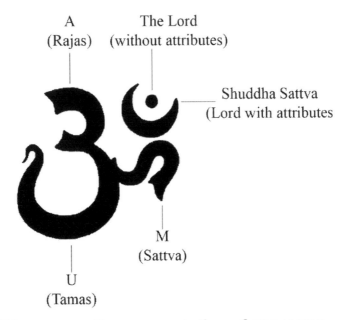

A
(Rajas)

The Lord
(without attributes)

Shuddha Sattva
(Lord with attributes

M
(Sattva)

U
(Tamas)

Diagrammatic representation of OM (AUM)

i) The Significance of "A" in AUM (OM)

The letter **A** represents:

Brahma (the creator) - it reminds us, that we should give thanks to our creator, for the provision of this beautiful world we live in.

Rg Veda - whibch deals with:

- Glorification of God via hymns.

- Virtuous conduct.

- Promotion of the welfare of all God's creation.

This Bhur Loka (this physical world) - is the place of our abode; it provides us with all our needs, for carrying out our activities of living. We are reminded, that we should demonstrate our appreciation of it, by taking good care of it so that present and future generation, can become beneficiaries of our thoughtfulness.

Rajo guna (Mode of activity and passion) - is one of the three qualities of the human mind. It is a reminder that those who are in the mode rajo guna (activity and passion), should utilize their wealth, fame and possessions to help the poor and disadvantaged in society.

Outcomes of those who meditate on the letter "A "of AUM (OM):

- Will gain enlightenment.

- Take birth as a human being, in which he or she lives a life based on Tapasya (austerities), Brahmacharya (self discipline) and Shraddha (faith in God).

- An individual of this nature, will attain (anubhavati) greatness (mahiman) among people.

Prashna Upanisad 5:3

Symbolism in Hinduism p 74

ii) The significance of the letter "U in AUM (OM)

The letter **U** represents the following:

Lord Shiva - who is the universal teacher and guru, who aids our spiritual growth, by removal of barriers to it.

Yajur Veda - which houses hymns to be used in religious rituals thus, aiding our spiritual growth.

Bhuvar Loka (Astral Plane) - this is the space between the earth and the sun. This planet is populated by celestial beings.

Tamo guna (mode of ignorance) - is one of the three (3) qualities of the human mind, which veils our Aatma (The Self/Soul) like a dense fog. It has the effect of apravrtti (making us dull), vimudha (deluded) and lacking in enthusiasm to seek our real nature i.e. we are Aatma (Self /Soul).

Outcome of those who meditate on the letter "U "of AUM (OM)

- Those who meditate on the letter **"U "of AUM (OM),** find contentment in participating in social welfare programmes such as planting trees and road construction.

- They achieve the world of the moon where, they enjoy the fruits of their labour.

- They are reborn into this world as male or female.

Prashna Upanisad 5:4 & 5:7

78

iii) The significance of M in AUM (OM)

The letter **M** represents the following:

Lord Vishnu (the sustainer of the universe), who makes our existence possible. Nothing in this universe, takes place without His grace. We are advised to perform all actions as a service to him.

Sama Veda - are verses of Rg Veda set to music. Some of its contents include sports, arts and literature. We are advised to utilise music, sports and literature to aid our spiritual growth.

Suvar Loka (spiritual plane) -is inhabited by those whose spiritual bank balance is made up of punya (merits). In comparison, earthly inhabitants have a spiritual bank balance of a mixture of punya (merits) and papa (sin).

We are reminded that activities dedicated to the Lord, will lead to the accumulation of punya (merits) which will lead to prasada buddhi (gaining the grace of The Lord)- the greatest merit.

Sattva (mode of goodness) - is a reminder that we should strive to develop shuddhi (purity) of manasa (thoughts), vak (speech) and kayena (actions) so that we are qualified to gain Aatma (Self/Soul) vidya (knowledge) i.e we are Aatma (Self/Soul)

Those who meditate on the letter "M "AUM (OM)

Those who meditate on the letter **"M"** of AUM (OM) attain the creator of the Universe - a world reserved for the spiritually knowledgeable.

Prashna Upanisad 5:7

79

Gunatita- one who has transcended the three qualities of the mind

Gunatita is a reminder that each spiritual aspirant, should make a conscious effort to rise above the qualities of the mind (mode of passion - rajas, mode of ignorance and laziness - tamas and mode of goodness - sattva), in order to experience our real nature i.e. the Aatma (self /soul). The Aatma (Self/Soul) and Brahman/Paramatman/Ishvar (The Lord) are one and the same.

Some useful aids to experience our real nature are:

- Anugraha -grace of The Lord is needed.

- Sarangathi -unconditional surrender to the Lord.

- Shraddha (faith) in Paramatma/ Brahman/Ishvar (The Lord) and the religious shastras (religious books) must be very strong.

- Provision of niskama karma (selfless service) in a spirit of karma phala tyaga (for the love of it) with an attitude of Vishnu arpanam astu (dedicating the work and its fruits to The Lord

- Practice seeing The Lord in everyone and everything you look at.

- Constant remembering of The Lord in manasa (thoughts) vak (words) and kayena (actions).

80

Reference

Swami Chinmayananda (2000) - Kathopanisad -C C M T, Mumbai, 400 072, India - 1:2:6

Swami Chinmayananda (1998) - Discourses on Taittiriya Upanisad- C C M T, Mumbai, 400 072, India- 1:8:1.

Swami Lokeswarananda (2009) - Katha Upanisad - Ramakrishna Mission Institute of Culture, Kolkata, 700 029, India -1:2:6.

Swami Lokeswarananda (2005) - Taittiriya Upanisad - Ramakrishna Mission Institute of Culture, Kolkata, 700 029, India -1:8:1.

Swami Prabhupada (1985) -The Bhagavadgita (As it is) - Bhaktivedanta Book Trust, Watford, Herts, WD2 4XA, UK- 7:8

Swami Dayananda Saraswati (2006) - Bhagavadgita (Home Study Course) - Arsha Vidya Gurukulum, Coimbatore, 641 108, India-7:8

Swami Chinmayananda (2010) -Prasnopanisad - C. C. M. T, Mumbai, 400 072, India. 5:7.

Swami Lokeswarananda (2011) - Prashna Upanisad - Ramakrishna Mission Institute of Culture, Kolkata, 700 029, India- 5:3, 5:4 and 5:7

Swami Nityananda (1996) -Symbolism in Hinduism - C. C. M. T, Mumbai, 400 072 India. P74.

81

Bibliography

Jairam B (1993) - Golden Teachings of Hinduism (Dharmik Prakash) - Dharmik Books, W.H. Inc, Canada- Pages 73-74.

Swami Lokeswarananda (2010) - Chandogya Upanisad - Ramakrishna Mission Institute of Culture, Kolkata, 700 029, India- 1:5, 1:7 and 1:9.

Swami Lokeswarananda (2005) - Mandukya Upanisad- Ramakrishna Mission Institute of Culture, Kolkata, 700 029, India- Upa 8,9,10 and 11(pages 64-76)

Swami Nityananda (1996) Symbolism in Hinduism –

C C M T, Mumbai, 400 072, India. P 73-74.

Swami Purnananda (1980) -Aum Hindutvam –
Swami Purnanda,
London, W12, UK- P 37-38.

6

Demi Gods and Nav Graha Devatas

1) Demi Gods

Who are the Demi Gods?

Devatas (Demi Gods) are celestial beings of high excellence i.e. their levels of merit are exceedingly high. They were once human beings.

Three levels of beings are:

i) Devatas (demi gods) - who are purely merit based (punya).

ii) Manusya (human beings) - are a mixture of merits (punyas) and sin (papas).

iii) Pashu (animal) are purely sin based (papas).

In the above three levels, Devatas (demi gods) are top of the tree.

Abode of the Devatas (Demi Gods)

The Devatas (demigods) live in swarga loka (celestial plane)

Some examples of Devatas (Demi Gods) and their responsibilities

Demi Gods	Responsibilities
Surya (Sun)	Source of illumination and heat
Chandra (moon)	Source of light at night and calmness
Vayu (Wind)	Manager of world wide circulation of wind
Varuna (water)	Overseer of water resources
Yama (restraint)	Administrator of death and justice
Kubera (wealth)	Universal treasurer
Indra (God of thunder and lightening)	Administrator of Heaven
Prajapati (Lord of people)	Propagator of life on earth
Agni (fire)	Agent of fire

<u>Source of power of the Devatas (Demi Gods)</u>

The source of the power of the Devatas (demi gods) is the Param (The Supreme) Aatma (The Lord).

Hinduism for All Chap 2: 5-6.

2) <u>Nava (nine) Grahas (Seize or take hold of)</u>

<u>What is the meaning of the words</u>:

a) Nava is defined as nine (9)

b) Grahas originates from the Sanskrit root **"grih "**which is explained as **"to seize or take hold of "**

The Nava (nine) Grahas) are living energies, which transmit waves of power, which have an influence on our awareness; in short, they are nine influences on our lives.

Role of the Nav (nine) Grahas (to seize or take hold of).

Sanskrit Name	English name	Functions of Each
i) Surya	Sun	- Spiritual father of mankind - Represents the Aatma (Soul/Self) - Covers the past and the future - Radiates light and love - Confers piety, truth and goodness (sattva)
ii) Chandra (Soma)	Moon	- Divine mother of human beings. - Administrator of akash (space) and the antah-karana (the mind). - Denotes the past - Demonstrates how we interacts with others. - Giver of sattva -piety, truth and goodness.

iii) Mangal (Commander in Chief	Mars	- Planet of energy, strength -Associated with success. -Aids research and Occupation. - Can be useful in promotion of yoga. -Is in the mode of Ignorance or tamo guna.
iv) Budha (The Prince)	Mercury	- Represents intellect, communication education as well as commonsense -Governs compassion - Is in the mode of passion or rajo guna.

v) Brihaspathi	Jupiter	-Ambassador for knowledge (jnana) and meditation. - Associated with creativity - Governs health - Is in the mode sattva – piety and goodness.
vi) Shukra	Venus	- Planet of love, comfort and beauty. -Source of inspiration and Vitality. -It is-in the mode of material energy
vii) Shani	Saturn	-Planet of extrovert tendencies and sense gratification. - Gives ability to attract the masses. - Can grant psychic powers. - Has been known to aid The process of of moksha(liberation).

viii) Rahu	Dragon's Head	- Associated with introverted tendencies. - Can promote spiritual growth and psychic abilities.
ix) Ketu	Dragon's tail	Creates doubt and disturbance.

The days of the week are named after seven (7) of Nava (Nine)

Grahas (influence on our lives)

Sanskrit names Planetary names	English names
1) Ravivar Surya (Sun or Itvar)	Sunday
2) Somvar Chandra (Moon)	Monday
3) Mangalvar Mangal (Mars)	Tuesday
4) Budhavar Budha (Mercury)	Wednesday
5) Brihaspativar Guruvar Brihaspati/Guru (Jupiter)	Thursday
6) Shukravar Shukra (Venus)	Friday
7) Shanivar Shani (Saturn)	Saturday

The blessings of Nava (nine) grahas (influence on our lives) are invoked before the following:

- Moving into a new house
- Starting up a new business
- Commencement of a marriage
- Beginning a course of education
- Applying for a job
- Going on a journey

Hinduism for All p24-25.

References

Bisnauth R. (1999) - Hinduism for All -APH Publishing, Delhi, 110 002, India. p 5-6 and 24-25

http:// www. trsiyengar. com/1d2l. shtml (2008)-navagraha the nine planets influence on earth

http://en. wikipedia. org/wiki/graha (2008)-navagraha

http://www. hinduwebsite. com/hinduism/navagrahas. asp (2008)-navagrahas, the planetary deities

http://www. webonautics. com/mythology/navagraha. Html (2008)-navagrahas

7

The Traya (3) Shariras (Bodies) and the Aatma (Self/Soul

According to Vedanta (end portion of the Vedas) there are Traya (three) Shariras (Bodies) these are:

i) Sthula (gross) **Sharira** (body).

ii)Suksma (subtle) **Sharira** (body).

iii) Karana (causal) **Sharira** (body).

Each Sharira (Body) will now be dealt with briefly

i) Sthula (gross) Sharira (body)

Definition of Sharira

That which disintegrates with the passage of time.

Defintion of Sthula (gross)

That which is perceived by the panch (five) indriyas (senses)of the individual concerned

Another name for Sthula (gross) Sharira (body)

This is referred to as Anna (food) maya (modification) Kosha (sheath)

What are the panch (five) indriyas (senses)?

The panc (five) indriyas (senses) are:

- Strotram (ears) to hear.

- Tvak (skin) to feel.

- Chaksu (eyes) to see.

- Rasana (tongue) to taste.

- Grhaanam (nose) to smell.

Composition of Sthula (gross) Sharira (body)

It is composed of the following elements:

- Akash (space)

- Vayu (air)

- Agni (fire)

- Apah (water)

- Prthvi or Bhumi (earth).

What happens at death of Sthula (gross) Sharira (body)

At death it disintegrates back into the five elements.

Some key points about Sthula (gross) Sharira (body)

i) **Birth**
It comes into being due to dharmic (virtuous) karmas (actions) at birth

ii) It is the medium or avenue through which, we conduct our transaction with the external world. This transaction is temporarily halted, during sleep and permanently at death.

The agencies of transactions with the outer world, are via the jnana (organs) Indriyas (senses) and these are:

- Shrotram (ears) - sound
- Tvak (skin) - touch
- Chaksu (eyes) -vision
- Rasana (tongue) -Taste
- Grhaanam (nose) - smell

Activities of living

The Sthula (gross) Sharira (body) enables us, to carry out our activities of living thus, it should be kept in a fit and healthy state to make this possible. Since the Aatma (Self or Soul) is in residence as Antaryami (The Lord within), it should be treated as a mandir (temple)

It is the abode for gaining experience

It is the abode for us to gain experience of our real nature i.e. Ayam (this) Aatma (Soul/Self) Brahma (The Lord) -

<u>Translation</u>

This soul is The Lord.

Sthula (gross) Sharira (body) from birth to death

- Asti -Foetal existence in the mother's womb.

- Jayate (birth) after nav (nine) mahine (months).

- Vardhate -growth in height and weight.

- Viparinamate -matures into adolescence and adult.

- Vyadhi -acquire disease as life progresses.

- Dosas -suffers from defects e.g. loss of body parts.

- Duhkham - (affected by pain) from adhyatmica sources (within the body), e.g. vyadhi (diseases) and dosas (defects) and the ageing process. It is also affected from adhibhautica factors e.g. from within this world e.g. poverty, theft and murder as well as, from adhidaivika -divine forces such as hurricane and earthquake.

- Apaksiyate - it decays or degenerates due to the ageing or disease processes. Vinashyati - death occurs, when the purpose for which this Sthula (gross) Sharira (body) came into existence, has been achieved.

Death of Sthula (gross) Sharira (body)

Death takes place when the purpose for which it has come into being has been realized (prarabdha Karma). Death is said to have occurred when the Suksma (subtle) Sharira (body) has departed from the Sthula (gross) Sharira (body).

Soon after death, the heat remaining in the Sthula (gross) Sharira (body), diffuses out thus it becomes cold to touch, bloated, emits gas or air and and decays. Once decay has taken place the inner space merges with the total external space.

2) Suksma (subtle) Sharira (body)

Definition of Suksma (subtle) Sharira (body)

Suksma (subtle) Sharira (body) derives its name, because it is not tangible as it is not available for sensory perception.

It pervades Sthula (gross) Sharira (body)

It pervades Sthula (gross) Sharira (body), maintaining physiological function and thereby life.

Birth of Suksma (subtle) Sharira (body)

It is born out of the the subtle form of the five elements before they were grossified i.e. not fully developed. The five elements are:
- Akash (space)
- Vayu (air)
- Agni (fire)
- Apah (water)
- Prthvi (earth)

Composition of Suksma (subtle) Sharira (body)

The composition are as follows:

i) Panch (five) jnana (organs) indriyas (sense)

- Srotram (ears) - hearing.

- Tvak (skin) - touch or feeling.

- Chaksu (eyes) - vision.

- Rasana (tongue) - taste.

- Ghraanam (nose) -smell.

ii) Panch (five) Karma (actions) Indriyas (organs)

- Vak (speech) - to communicate.

- Pani (hands) - for lifting and holding.

- Pada (legs) - for locomotion.

- Payu (anus) - to remove waste products of body metabolism e.g. urine and faeces.

- Upasthani (genitals) for procreation.

iii) Panch (five) pranas (vital airs)

- Prana - is the life force, which controls and regulates the activities, of the jnana (organs) indriyas (sense). The jnana (organs) indriyas (senses) are srotram (ears), tvak (skin), chaksu (eyes), rasana (tongue) and grhaanam (nose).

- Apana aids removal of the waste products of body metabolism, thus aiding the maintenance of a healthy body.

- Samana -makes ingestion, digestion and assimilation of nutrients or food into the body possible.

- Vyana - aids distribution of nutrition and vital components, such as oxygen, hormones, enzymes, antibodies, antitoxins, which are vital for cellular survival. It also facilitates removal of cellular waste products.

- Udana - makes reflex action such as vomiting, sneezing, crying and burping possible.

iv) Antah-karana (The inner organs)

These are composed of:

a) Antah-karana (the mind) - is a constant flow of thoughts. It is the agent of general thinking, indecisiveness and emotion.

b) Buddhi (intellect) is the agency of discrimination and makes decisions based on objective assessment and analysis.

c) Chitta (memory) -deals with storage and recall.

d) Ahamkara (ego)- gives a sense of I-ness and My-ness or egoism.

Koshas (Sheaths) located within Suksma (subtle) Sharira (body)

- Pranamaya (life force) kosha (sheath) - makes physiological functions possible.

- Manomaya (mental) kosha (sheath) - covers psychological aspect of the person.

- Vijnanamaya (Intellect) kosha (sheath) -deals with the intellectual make up of the individual.

  The above-mentioned koshas (sheaths) will be commented on in more details in a separate chapter.

3) Karana (causal) Sharira (body)

Definition of Karana (causal) Sharira (body)

It is shapeless, sizeless and beginning less; since it is indescribable, it cannot be grasped by the mind.

Its responsibility

It is responsible for the creation of Sthula (gross) and Suksma (subtle) Shariras (bodies).

It is the subtlest of the traya (three) Shariras (bodies)

It is the subtlest of the traya (three) shariras (bodies) and, it pervades the Suksma (subtle) and the Sthula (gross) Shariras (bodies).

Karana (causal) sharira (body) and avidya (ignorance)

The karana (causal) sharira (body) is in a state of avidya (ignorance) of its real nature i.e. ayam (this) Aatma (self or soul) is Brahman (The Lord). This avidya (ignorance) has led to identification with sthula (gross) and suksma (subtle) shariras (bodies).

Kosha (sheath) located within Karana (causal) Sharira (body)

Karana (causal) Sharira (body) houses anandamaya (bliss) kosha (sheath).

References

Chaitanya S (1993) - Tattva Bodha of Sakaracarya- C C M T, Mumbai,400 072, India - P24-26

Swami Chinmayananda (2011) - Aatmabodha - C C M T, Mumbai, 400 072, India - V 12,13. 14.

Swami Dayananda Saraswati (2004)- Tattva Bodha - Arsha Vidya Gurukulum, Coimbatore, 641 108, Tamil Nadu, India - P 13-14.

Swami Dayananda Saraswati (1997)- Viveka Cudamanini (Talks on 108 selectedVerses)-Sri Gangadhar Trust, Rishikesh, 249 201, UP, India- VN27 - 29.

Swami Tejomayananda (2001) - Tattvah Bodh of Sri Adi Shankaracarya - C C M T, Mumbai, 400 072, India- P32-45.

8

The Panch (five) Koshas s(sheath) and The Aatma (Self)

Definition of a sheath (kosha)

A sheath (kosha) is a covering, which is used to house or cover something e.g. the cocoon of a silkworm or a sword's scabbard.

Swami Harshananda (1995)

Definition of the five (panc) Sheaths (koshas)

"Those factors of our personality which cover or hide the Aatma (Self or Soul) like a sheath covering a sword ".

Swami Harshananda (1995)

The five (panc) sheaths (koshas) and avidya (ignorance)

According to Swami Shudhabodhananda (1994), the panc (five) koshas (sheaths) seems to act as a covering, of the Aatma (Self or Soul). He attributes this unreal covering, to our impaired vision which is brought about, by avidya (ignorance) of our real nature which is **Aatma (Self/ Soul) is Brahman (The Lord).**

What are the five (panc) sheaths (koshas)?

The five (panc) sheaths (koshas) are:

i) **Sthula** (gross/physical) **sharira** (body) **or annamaya**
    (food) **kosha** (sheath)

ii) **Pranamaya** (life force or vital air) **kosha** (sheath).

iii) **Manomaya** (mental) **kosha** (sheath).

iv) **Vijnanamaya** (intelligence) **kosha** (sheath)

v) **Anandamaya** (bliss) **kosha** (sheath).

i) What is annamaya (food) kosha (sheath)?

The word **maya** in **annamaya** refers to modification or
change i.e. it is born of food, grows by food alone and
returns to the earth, in the form of food at death.

List the composition of the annamaya (food) kosha
(sheath)

Annamaya (food) kosha (sheath), is made up of the the
panc (five) elements, after grossification; they are:

- Space (akash)

- Air (vayu)

- Fire (agni

- Water (apah)

- Earth (prthvi)

103

What is the significance of the panc five) elements?

- Sthula (gross/ physical) sharira (body) occupies akash (space).

- Respiration (inspiration and expiration) is made possible by vayu (air).

- Agni (fire) maintains body temperature.

- The body is made up of apah (water) and its percentage, is determined by age. Apah (water) is responsible for its hydration level.

- Sthula Sharira (the human body) is made up of minerals which comes from prthvi (earth).

ii) Pranamaya (Vital air) kosha (sheath)

Definition of pranamaya (vital air or life force) kosha (sheath)

Pranamaya (vital or life force) kosha (sheath), is a combination of panc (five) pranas (vital airs), and the karma (of action) indriyas (organs).

b) State the composition of the Pranamaya (vital air or life force) and list their function

Pranamaya (vital air or life force) kosha (sheath) is made up of panc (five) vital airs (physiological functions) and panc (five) karma (of action) indriyas (organs).

What are the names of the five vital airs are:

a) Prana

It is the agency responsible for breathing in (inspiration of oxygen) and breathing out (expiration of carbon dioxide)

b) Apana

Apana - is responsible for the removal of waste products of body metabolism e.g. urine, faeces and carbon dioxide which are toxic.

c) Vyana aids circulation of the blood which makes it possible, for vital essentials such as oxygen, nutrition, hormones and enzymes, to be available to maintain cellular health.

d) Samana

Samana is the agency responsible for the following:

- Ingestion or taking in food into the digestive system.
- Digestion or breaking down of large particles of food into smaller ones.
- Assimilation or absorption of digested food which aids a positive health.

e) Udana

Udana aids reflex action such as:

- Crying
- Sweating

- Vomiting
- Burping

Some key points of pranamaya (vital air or life force) kosha sheath))

- It is essential for health promotion and maintenance

- The panc (five) pranamaya (vital air or life force) links and energises suksma (subtle) Sharira (body) and sthula (the gross or physical) sharira (body).

- It pervades and gives life to the sthula (gross or physical) sharira (body).

  Its absence result in death as we know it.

The panc (five) karma (of action) indriyas (organs) are

- Vak (speech) - responsible for communication.

- Pani (hands) -aids holding and grasping.

- Pada (legs/feet) -makes locomotion possible.

- Payu (anus) - evacuates faeces.

- Upasthani (genitals) - deals with procreation.

iii) Manomaya (Mental) kosha (Sheath)

Definition of manomaya (mental) kosha (sheath)

Manomaya (mental) kosha (sheath) is a combination of:

a) The manas (mind)

b) The panc (five) jnana (perception) indriyas (organs of)

Tatva Bodha p 34-37
Tatvabodha p26-28
Panchadsashi p84-8
Tattva Bodhah p 52-60
Panchadashi 68,69,71

a) The manas (mind)

Definition of manas (the mind)

Swami Tejomayananda ((2010) sees manas (the mind) as a flow of thoughts at a terrific speed. Swami Lokeswarananda (2010) goes on to add that manas (the mind) is the controller of the senses, that it (the mind) is the daivam (divine) chaksu (eyes), because Aatma (the Self or Soul) sees through it.

b) The panc (five) jnana (perception) (indriyas (organs of)

The five (panc) organs (indriyas) of knowledge or perception (jnana) are:

107

- Ears (strotram) - hearing.
- Skin (tvak)   - touch.
- Eyes (chaksu) - vision.
- Tongue (rasana) - taste.
- Nose (grhanam) - smell.

Identification of the Aatma (Self or Soul) with manomaya (mental)kosha (sheath)

When Aatma (Self or Soul) identifies itself with the manomaya (mental) kosha (sheath), the following feelings are experienced:

- I am happy.
- I am sad.
- I feel good.

iv) Vijnana (intelligence) Kosha (Sheath)

Definition of vijnanamaya (intelligence) Kosha (Sheath)

Vijnanamaya (intelligence) kosha (sheath), is the domain of rational decision making.

Composition of vijnanamaya (intelligence) kosha (sheath).

This kosha (sheath) is made up as follows:

- Buddhi (intellect)
- Panc (five) jnana (sense) indriyas (organs)

Definition of buddhi (intellect)

The buddhi (intellect) is the faculty of rational decision making made possible, by viveka (its ability to discriminate) and by vichar (deliberation on the positives and negatives issues before it).

Harshananda (1995) sees the buddhi (intellect), as one of the four components of the antah-karana (mind). The four components are manas (mind), buddhi (intellect), citta (memory) and ahamkara (ego).

Tejomayananda (2001) views buddhi (the intellect), as the place of one's values which is useful in making sense of our outer world.

Role of the buddhi (intellect)

i) It controls annamaya (food), pranamaya (vital airs) and manomaya (mental) koshas (sheaths).

ii) Being suksma (subtle), it pervades the above-mentioned koshas (sheaths).

iii) Attachment to the body (sharira) due to ignorance (avidya) of its real nature i.e. Aatma (Self/Soul) is Brahman (The Lord) makes it believes that it is:

- It is limited.
- It is the doer.

Thus it thinks that:

- Iam tall.
- I am hungry.
- Iam happy.

Swami Tejomayananda 2001

The Panch (five) jnana (organs) indriyas (perception) are:

- Strotram (ears) -deals with hearing.
- Tvak (skin) -deals with touch.
- Chaksu (eyes)- responsible for vision.
- Rasana (tongue)- makes taste possible.
- Grhanam (nose)-aids the sense of smell.

v) Ananda maya (bliss) Kosha (sheath)

Definition of the anandamaya (bliss) kosha (sheath)

This kosha (sheath) which is of the nature of avidya (established in ignorance), which is in the form of the karana (causal) sharira (body), is of sattva (impure mode of goodness). and united with vrittis (modifications).

110

What is impure sattva?

Impure sattva (malinasattva) is a combination of the sattva (mode of goodness) rajas (activity/passion) and tamas (dullness).

What are vrittis (modifications)?

Vrittis are thought modifications and they are:

i) Priya Vritti - is the joy on seeing a dear person or object.

ii) Moda Vritti - refers to the joy one gets from possessing the object of one's desire; this joy is greater than that experienced in priya vritti.

iii) Pramoda Vritti - is the joy one obtains from the desired object. This joy is greater than that experienced in moda vritti.

Ananda maya (bliss) kosha (sheath) and the karana (causal) sharira (body)

It is called karana (causal) sharira (body) and, it is the subtlest as well as the most pervasive of all the koshas (sheaths).

Reference

Swami Harshananda (1995)- A Dictionary of Advaita Vedanta - Ramakrishna Math Bangalore, 500 069, India.

Chaitanya S (1993) - Tattva Bodha of Sankaracarya - C
C M T, Mumbai,400 072, India - P 34-38.

Swami Lokeswarananda (2010) -Chandogya Upanisad -
Ramakrishna Mission Institute of Culture, Kolkata, 700
029, India-8:12:5.

Swami Dayananda Saraswati (2004) - Tattvabodhah -
Arsha Vidya Gurukulum Coimbatore, 641 108, India- P
26-30.

Swami suddhabodhananda (1994) - Panchadashi
(Discovering your Innate Greatness - Sri Visweswar
Trust, Bombay, 400 056, India-Chapter 1: P 84-87.

Swami Tejomayananda (2001) - Tattva Bodhah
(Shri Aadi Shankaracarya) -CCMT, Mumbai, 400 072,
India- P 52-60.
Swami Tejomayananda (2006)- Tattva Viveka - C C MT,
Mumbai, 400 072, India- Chapter 1: P 68,69, and 71.

Swami Tejomayananda (2010)- Amtitabindu Upanisad
(A drop of Immortality) –C C M T, Mumbai, 400 072,
India - P 14.

9

The Lord, Maya, Prakrti, and The Lord

Maya

Definition of Maya

Tattva Viveka verse 16 defines maya in the following manner:

Sattva -shuddhya vishuddhibhyam maya avidye ca te mate, maya bimba vashikrtya taamsyatsarvajna eeshvarah.

Sattva - shuddya (from the predominantly pure sattva) avishudhibhyam (and the impure sattva combined with rajas and tamas) maya avidye ca te mate (are known as maya and avidya respectively);

maya bimba (one who is reflected in maya) vashikrtya (having controlled) tam (that maya) syat (becomes) sarvajna (the omniscient) Ishvara (The Lord)

Translation

Pure Prakrti with predominant sattva is called maya. Sattva combined with rajas and tamas (impure) is referred to as avidya.

Two other definitions of Maya offered by Swami Tejomayananda (1993) are:

i) Ma - to create

    Ya - that which

Translation

That which creates is maya.

ii) Ma - not

    Ya - that which

Translation

That which is not is maya.

Maya is called devatma shakti

Maya (that which creates or that which is not) is called devatma (The Lord) shakti (power), because it belongs to The Lord and exists because of Him.

Shetashvatara Upanisad V3.

Maya has three (tri) qualities (gunas)

These are:

i) Sattva - balance, knowledge, purity.

ii) Rajas - activity, energy, passion and restlessness.

114

iii) Tamas - dullness which acts at the intellectual level as a veiling agent, rendering the intellect incapable of knowing the Self/Soul (Aatma).

Om catuhshloka - Bhagavata p 18.
Viveka Cudamani p 106.

Maya is hidden by the three (tri) qualities (gunas)

Maya (that which creates and that which is not) is hidden (niguudham) by the veil of its own qualities (gunas). These qualities (gunas) are:

i) Sattva - balance, knowledge and purity.

ii) Rajas - energy, activity, restlessness and passion.

iii)Tamas - dullness which acts at the intellectual level as a veiling agent, rendering the intellect incapable of knowing the Self/Soul (Aatma).

Avidya
What is avidya?

When the three (tri) qualities (gunas - sattva, rajas and tamas) are mixed, they are called ignorance (avidya). This ignorance (avidya) acts as an obstruction thus, the Self or Soul is not experienced. Ignorance (avidya) is the causal (karana) body (sharira)

Tattva Viveka V16 p 37.

Powers of ignorance (avidya)

Ignorance (avidya) which is a combination of balance, knowledge and purity (sattva), energy, passion and restlessness (rajas), and dullness (tamas), is impure has two powers which are:

i) Covering or hiding (avarana) which veils the Self/Soul (Aatma).

ii) Projection (viksepa) which creates a false identity e.g. I am the body - mind- intellect.

Amrtabindu Upanisad p58.

Maya and creation

Gita 9:10 emphasises the creative nature of Maya thus:

Maya adhyaksena prakrtih, sooyate sacara-acaram.

Maya (by me) adhyaksena (direction) prakrti (material nature), sooyate (creates) sa (both) cara - acaram (the world of the moving and non-moving).

Translation

By my direction, prakrti or maya creates the world of the moving and non-moving. Shevtashvatara Upanisad 4:10 p 177 is supportive of this statement.

Prakrti

What is prakrti

Kr   - to do

Krti - done or creation

Prakrti - exalted creation.

Prakrti and creation

It is the primordial (existing from the beginning of time) cause of the world. It is also the inherent creative power of The Lord.

Tattva Vivekah V15.

It (prakrti - nature or material cause) can create in the presence of The Lord (Brahman).

Pancadashi Chapter1: v5: p52

Types of Prakrti

There are two types of Prakrti. These are:

i) Para (superior) Prakrti

This Para (superior) Prakrti is the Lord (Brahman) who is:

- Samagram (absolute) Sat (Existence).

- Samagram (absolute) Cit (Consciousness).

117

- Samagram (absolute) Ananda (bliss).

- Aksara (indestructible).

- Parama (limitless).

- Avyaya (changeless).

- Ksetrajna (knower of the field).

ii) Apara (inferior) Prakrti

Apara (inferior) Prakrti consists of traya (three) gunas (qualities of the mind. The qualities of the mind (gunas) are:

- Sattva - goodness and purity.

- Rajas -activity, restlessness and passion.

- Tamas -laziness and ignorance.

Apara (inferior) Prakrti is the external manifestation of the Supreme (Param) Lord (Ishvar). It is the cause of material creation and it is referred to as the field of activities (ksetra).

The Lord maya and prakrti

Shwetashvatarara Upannisad 4:10 demonstrate the following links with The Lord, maya and prakrti:

Mayam tu prakrtim vidyan mayinam ca maheshvaram,
Tasya avayavabhutaih vyptaam sarvam idam jagat.

Mayam (maya) tu (surely) prakrtim (nature) vidyan (know)
mayinam (The Lord of maya) ca (and) Maheshvaranam (The Lord);
tasya (His) avayavabhutaih (body), vyaptam (filled) sarvam (all) idam (this) jagat (world).

Translation

Maya and prakrti are one and the same; sometimes it is called maya and at other times, it is called prakrti. Prakrti or maya is the material cause of the world. Maheshvara (The Great Lord) is the body of this world.

The Lord is mayavi

The Lord (Brahman) is the master, controller and wielder of maya or prakrti.

Shwetashvatara Upanisad 4;10; p176

References

Swami Lokeswarananda (2005)- Shewtashwatara Upanisad - Ramakrishna Misssion Institute of Culture, Kolkata, 700 029, India- Verse3: P 15.

Swami Dayananda Saraswati (1997) - Viveka Cudamani – Sri Gangadhareswar Trust, Rishikesh, 249 201, India- Verse 31: P 106.

Swami Dayananda Saraswati (2006) -Bhagavad Gita (Home Study Course) - Arsha Vidya Gurukulum, Coimbatore, 641 108, India- 9:14.

Swami Suddhabodhananda (1994)- Panchadashi
(Discovering Your Innate Greatness) - Sri Visweswar
Trust, Bombay, 400 056, India- Chapter1: Verse 5: P 52.

Swami Tejomayananda (1993) - Catusloki Bhagavata –
C C MT, Mumbai, 400 072, India- P 16-18
Swami Tejomayananda (2001) - Shetashvatara Upanisad
- C C M T, Mumbai,400 072, India- 1:3: P14 and 4: 10: P
176.

Swami Tejomayananda (2006) -Tattva Viveka
(Panchadashi) -C C M T, Mumbai,400 072, India-
Chapter 1: Verse15: P 32-35 and Verse 16: P 36-37.

Swami Tejomayananda (2010) - Amritabindu Upanisad -
C C M T, Mumbai, 400 072, India- P:58.

120

10

Jiva, Body, Birth and Death

This chapter is organized into four sections; these are:

i) Jiva

ii) Body

iii) Birth

iv) Death

i) <u>Jiva</u>

<u>Definition of Jiva</u>

Swami Harshananda (1995) defines jiva, as a living being in
a state of bondage and undergoing transmigration. He goes on to add that jiva is a reflection of pure conscious (Chaitanya) in the intellect (buddhi). Gita 15:7 defines jiva as follows:

Mam eva amsha jiva loke, jiva-bhootah sanaatanah

Mama (my) eva (only) amsha (part or fragment) jiva (the individual), loke (world) jiva (living) bhutah (being).

<u>Translation</u>

In the individual's world, an eternal part of Me exists as the Jiva.

Transmigration explained

The cycle of births and deaths or transmigration is referred to as **samsara** (to move).

The real nature of Jiva

Being a fragment (amsha)of The Lord, jiva (a living being in

a state of bondage and undergoing transmigration) is:

- Samagram (absolute) Sat (existence).

- Samagram (absolute) Cit (consciousness/awareness).

- Samagram (absolute) Ananda (bliss).

Jiva is gender free

The jiva (living in a state of bondage and undergoing transmigration) is gender free and this is made clear by Shetashvatara Upanisad 5:10:

Na eva stri pumaan-esa na ca eva aayam na pumsakah, yat yat   shariram aadatte tena sa raksyate.

Na (not) eva (surely) stri (female) na (not) pumaan (male) esah (this), na (not) ca (and) eva (surely) ayam (this) na pum sakah (eunuch);

Yat yat (whichever) shariram (body) adatte (assumes), tena tena (by those very bodies) sa raksyate (it is known or protected).

Translation

This jiva is surely not female, nor male and not a eunuch. It assumes different forms, as a result of its previous karma or action and it is known by those forms.

Shvetashvatara Upanisad (5:10).

Additional translation

The Aatma (Self/Soul/God) even as an individual is neither a male, female nor eunuch. Though the Aatma (Self/Soul) is Samagram (absolute) Sat (existence)), Samagram (absolute) Cit (Consciousness/awareness) and Samagram (absolute) Ananda (Bliss) it **is unconditioned by any body.** He (The Lord) manifests in all forms of life.

The individual jiva (embodied living being) has no form but takes on or assumes a form of its own. Just as a man is not the house he lives in, similarly, the jiva (living embodied being) is not the body it is encased in.

Jiva and this physical body

Because of previous action (karma), a given physical body comes into existence i.e. it is born. Due to ignorance (avidya)of it's real nature i.e. it is Aatma (Self/Soul), that atma (Self/Soul) is Param (Supreme) Aatma (Lord) and

123

Aatma (Self/Soul) is Samagram (absolute) Sat (existence), Samagram (absolute) Cit (consciousness/awareness and Samagram (absolute) and Ananda (bliss), the jiva (embodied living being) identifies itself with the physical/gross (sthula) body (sharira - that which disintegrates).

As long as ignorance (avidya) of one's real nature i.e. Aatma (the Self/Soul) and Param (Supreme) Aatma (The Lord) are one and the same exists, the jiva (embodied livng being) will be caught up, in countless cycles of births and deaths or transmigration (samsara).

As soon as the jiva (embodied living being) realizes that his real nature is the Self/Soul (Aatma),), all his actions (karmas) gets exhausted at a stroke. This is freedom from limitation (moksha).

Mundako upanisad 2:2;7

Jiva and extraversion

Katha Upanisad 2:4:1 makes this statement about the jiva (embodied living being):

Paraanci khani vyatrnat svayambhooh, tasmaat paran pashyati na antaraAatman,

Kashcit dheerah pratyag Aatmaan eksat, aavrtta caksur amrtatvam icchan.

124

Paranci (going outward) khani (the senses) vyatrnat (created with defects) swayambhooh (Brahma-The Creator),

tasmat (therefore) paraan (external universe) pashyati (sees) na (not) antar Aatman (the internal self); kaschit (some) dhirah (wise person) pratyagAatmanam (the sel/soul within) eksat (sees), avrtta (turned inside) caksuh(eyes)amrtatvam (immortality) icchan (being desirous).

Translation

The creator of the world (Brahma), created the senses with extraverted or outgoing tendencies; thus, man by constantly looking out, perceives the external world and not the Aatma (Self/Soul) within.

Some wise person desirous of immortality, turn the senses away from sense objects and focus on the internal, where the Aatma (Self/Soul) is experienced.

Jiva and ignorance

Due to ignorance (avidya), of its real nature i.e. the Aatma (Self/Soul) is real and it is the same as Param (Supreme) Aatma (The Lord), that the body/mind/intellect (ksetram) is time bound, yet, jivas (embodied living beings) get immersed in the time bound world of objects on account of, the senses being extraverted (paraagdarshina) which result in actions (karmas) being performed to gain them.

Thus, jivas (embodied living beings) are helplessly caught in a vicious circle of actions (karmas) and sense enjoyments (bhoga) called the cycle of births and deaths or transmigration (samsara).

Tattva Vivekah 1:30 emphasizes this point very nicely:

Nadyam keeta ivaavartaad aavartaataram ashu te,

Vrajanto janmano janma labhante na eva nirvrtim.

Nadhyam (in the river) keeta (insects) iva (like) avartat (from one whirlpool) avartaantaram (to another whirlpool) aashu (fast) te (those jivas),

Vrajanto (keep moving) janmano (from one birth) janma (to next birth) labhante (attain) na (never) eva (indeed) nirvrtim (peace).

Translation

Like insects fallen into a river, keep going from one whirlpool to another, similarly, jivas (embodied living beings) keep going from one birth to another thus, they never attain peace.

Effects of avidya and its products on the Jiva

Definition of avidya

Lacking in knowledge of one's real nature i.e. we are Aatma (Self/Soul), that Aatma (Self/Soul) and Param (Supreme) Aatma (Lord) are one and the same, implies ignorance and this is termed **avidya** or **ajnana.**

126

Results of avidya

The jiva (embodied living being) is filled with lack of knowledge or ignorance (avidya), the products of which are:

- Anisha (feeling of helplessness).

- Shoka (grief)

The effects of the products of lack of knowledge or ignorance (avidya) are:

- Kama -desire.

- Krodhah -anger.

- Lobha -greed.

- Moha -delusion.

- Mada -pride.

- Matsarya -envy.

- Ragas -likes/attachments.

- Dvesas -dislikes/hatred.

- Ahamkara -ego.

Jiva and samsara

Definition of jiva

A jiva is an embodied living being, in a state of bondage and undergoing transmigration.

Swami Harshananda (1995)

Definition of samsara

Samsara comes from the root "**sr**" "**to move** "and refers to the cycle of births and deaths or transmigration of the Self/Soul.

Swami Harshananda (1995)

What is the cause of samsara?

The cause of samsara (cycle of births and deaths), is due to attachment of the jivas (embodied living being), to the ksetram (body/mind/intellect complex) and forgetfulness of its real nature i.e. the Aatma (Self/Soul) and Brahman/ParamAatman (The Lord) are one and the same.

How to overcome samsara

Samsara (the cycle of births and deaths or transmigration of the Soul) can be overcome by:

128

i) Grace of The Lord (anugraha)

Without the grace of The Lord (anugraha) success in any field of endeavour is not possible. One's supplication should possess humility and sincerity.

ii) Possessing a burning desire to overcome samsara

The seeker must be consumed by an unbearable desire to overcome samsara (the cycle of births and deaths).

iii) Seek to obtain prepatory qualifications to overcome samsara

These qualifications are:

a) Vivekah (discrimination) i.e. know the difference between:

- Absolute existence (Sat) and impermanent existence (Asat)

- The Self / Soul (Aatma) and the body/mind/intellect (anaatma)

- Eternal (nitya) and the non-eternal (anitya).

- Virtuous conduct (Dharma) and non-virtuous conduct (adharma).

b) Vairagya (detachment) is giving up attachment for the impermanent which are:

- Non-absolute existence (asat)

- Body/mind/intellect complex (anatma)

- Non-eternal (anitya) which are objects of the senses.

- Sinful conduct (adharma)

Having given up the impermanent, one should practice turning within to experience one real nature i.e. the Aatma (Self or Soul).

c) Shamadi Satka (group of six)

i) Shama (mastery of the mind)

Knowledge takes place in the mind thus, it is important to gain mastery of it, so that it can focus on gaining knowledge (vidya) of the Self (Aatma). Some useful aids to gain shama (mastery of the mind) are:

- Prarthna (Prayer).

- Japa (repitition of The Lord's name (s).

- Shastra (study of the scripture).

- Thinking (bhavana) positive (paksa) instead of negative (prati)

Some benefits of shama (mastery of the mind are:

- Strong will power

- Blissfulness

- Peacefulness

ii) Dama (mastery of the senses)

Dama (mastery of the senses) makes it possible, for one to focus on experiencing one's real nature i.e. The Aatma (Self/Soul). It is to be noted thatBrahman or Paramatman (The Lord) and Aatma (Self/Soul) are one and the same. Some exercises to gain dama (mastery of the senses) are:

- Vision - practice seeing the Lord in everyone and everything you look at.

- Breath - let each breath remind you that you are the Lord (aham Brahmasmi).

- Speech - let your words be truthful (satyam), auspicious (shivam), beautiful (sundaram), sweet (madhuram) and blissful (anandam).

- Hearing - practice hearing the transcendental glories and pastimes of The Lord in all sounds.

- Touch - utilise this body/mind/intellect (ksetram) to work for the lord.

iii) Uparati - is the removal of one's self, from potential and stimuli which disturbs the healthy balance of the mind.

iv) Titiksa - is the cheerful acceptance of the pairs of opposites, as the grace of The Lord as an aid to one's spiritual growth. Some examples of pairs of opposites are:

- Praise and blame
- Love and hate
- Success and failure
- Wealth and poverty
- Health and ill health
- Happiness and distress
- Heat and cold

v) Shraddha (faith) must be demonstrated in the shastra (scripture)), the guru (spiritual master) and The Aatma (Self/ Soul).

vi) Samadhana (Concentration) - is joyful capacity to contemplate and concentrate on experiencing one's self/soul (Aatma) at all times,

d) Mumuksutva (desire for liberation) - is a burning, passionate hunger and desire to experience one's real nature i.e. we are Aatma (The Self/Soul) and Aatma

(Self/Soul) and Brahman or Paramatman (The Lord) are one and the same.

Benefits of gaining these prepatory qualifications to overcome samsara

One who has successfully gained the fourfold qualifications of **a) vivekah**(discrimination), **b) vairagya** (detachment) **c) shamadi satka** -group of six (Shama - mastery of the mind, dama - mastery of the senses, uparati -removal of one's self from sources of mental irritation, titiksa -forbearance,
shraddha - faith and samadahana- concentration) and) **d) mumuksutva**- desire for liberation, will be blessed with a pure mind (antah-karana shuddhi).

Purity of mind (antah-karana shuddhi) gives self control to the spiritual aspirant (sadhaka) which makes it possible for him or her to see (pashyati) The Lord (Ishan) as himself or herself.
This experience releases the seeker from the world of sorrow (vita shoka) and is called freedom from limitations (moksha).

Mundakopanisad 3:1:2

References

Swami Chinmayananda (1997) - Mundakopanisad - C C
M T, Mumbai,400 072, India - 3;1:2

Swami Chinmayananda (2000) - Kathopanisad (A
dialogue with death) - C C M T, Mumbai, 400 072, India
- 2:41.

Swami Harshananda (1995) - A Dictionary of Advaita
Vedanta- Ramakrishna Math, Bangalore, 560 019, India

Swami Lokeswarananda (2005) - Shetashvatara
Upanisad -Ramakrishna Mission Institute of Culture,
Kolkata,700 029, India 5:10

Swami Lokeswarananda (2008) -Mundaka Upanisad
- Ramakrishna Mission Institute of Culture, Kolkata,
700 029, India - 3:1:2.

Swami Lokeswarananda (2009)- Katha Upanisad
- Ramakrishna Mission Institute of Culture, Kolkata,
700 029, India - 2:41.

Swami Prabhupada (1985) -The Bhagavadgita (as it is) –
Bhaktivedanta Book Trust Watford, Herts, WD2 4XA,
UK - 15:7.

Swami Dayananda Saraswati (2006) - Mundako
Upanisad -Arsha Vidya Centre Research and Publication,
Chennai, 600 004, India - 2:2:7 and 3:1:2.

Swami Dayananda Saraswati (2006) – Bhagavadgita (Home Study Course) -Arsha Vidya Gurukulum, Coimbatore, 641 108, India -15:7.

Swami Tejomayananda (2010) - Shetashvatara Upanisad – C C M T, Mumbai, 400 072, India – 5:10

Swami Tejomayananda (2006) - Tattva Vivekah – C C M T, Mumbai, 400 072, India - Chapter1:1:30.

Swami Suddhabodhananda (1994)- Panchdashi (Discovering Your innate greatness) - Greatness Sri Viswesar Trust, Bombay,400 006, India - chapter1: 1:30 Bombay, 400 056,

2) The Body,

The lord (Brahman or Paramatma) the Soul/Self (jivatma) and the body (sharira)

Both the Supreme (Param) Lord (atma) and the Self/Soul (embodied living being- jivatma) reside in this body (shariram). The Self/Soul (embodied living being - jivatma) is dependent on The Supreme (Param) Lord (atma) for its existence.

The Supreme (Param) Lord (atma) is all knowing (sarvjna) whereas The Self/Soul (embodied living being - jivatma) is limited in knowledge (ajna).

The Self/Soul (Aatma) and identification with the body (sharira)

The Self/Soul (Aatma) is the knower of the body-mind-intellect complex (ksetram). When it identifies with the body (shariram - that which decays) It says, this is my body.

This affinity of the imperishable knower (kstrejna) with the perishable body (sharira), is called the embodied Self/Soul (shariri - jiva).

This body is referred to as a field

Gita 13:1 substantiates the above statement in this manner:

Idam shariram ksetram iti abhidhiyate.

Idam (this) shariram (body) ksetram (the field) iti (thus) abhidhiyate (is called).

Translation

This body is referred to as a field.

Additional translation

One sows the seeds of actions (karmas) in this field. Some actions (karmas) are for the good or welfare of society; in the fullness of time, they yield positive outcomes (punyas). Other actions (karmas) are unethical and wrong and they in time, yield fruits of negativity (sin).

This body is unreal

This body is (sharira) is unreal for several reasons; these are:

i)It did not exist before birth nor will it exist after death (Gita 2:16)

Na asatah vidyate bhaavah, na abhaavah vidyate satah;

Ubhayoh api drstah antah, tu anayoh tattva darshibhih

Na (never) asatah (for the non-existence or unreal) vidyate (there is) bhaavah (being), na (never) abhaavah (non- being) vidyate (there is) satah (for the real or eternal);
 ubhayoh (of the two) api (also) drsta (is seen or observed) antah (conclusion or ultimate truth, tu (indeed)

anyoh (of them) tattva (of the truth) darshibhih (seen or knower of the truth).

Translation

The unreal has no existence where as the real, never ceases to be. The final truth of these two, has been perceived by seers or knowers of the truth.

Additional translation

The Aatma (Self/Soul) is real and never ceases to be. It existed before the birth of this body (sharira), exists now and will exist after the death of this body (sharira).

A person who recognizes the differences between the real (Sat) and the unreal (asat), is seen as wise or enlightened (dhira). The wise or enlightened person (dhira) does not grieve at the demise of the body (sharira) or the world (jagat).

ii) All births result in death (Gita 2:20 - modified)

As soon as birth takes place, modifications of this perishable body (sharira) begins. The process of modifications is:

- Jayate -a perishable body (shariram) is born (jayate).

- Asti -it exists.

- Vardhate -it grows.

- Vyadhi -it picks up disease (s).

- Dosa-defects or handicaps become apparent with time.

- Apaksiyate-wear and tear of the body (sharira) takes place with ageing.

- Duhkham -Pain result from disease, defects and wear and tear.

- Jara -the body ages with the passage of time.

- Mrtyu -death finally arrives and it is destroyed (vinashyati)

iii) <u>The following names indicates the unreal nature of this body (sharira)</u>

Some names of this body are:

- Sharira -that which decays.
- Ksara - perishable.
- Ksetra - non-self i.e. the field of action.
- Apara prakrti - lower or inferior.
- Deha - that which is to be burnt.

References

Nath P. V. (2002)- Tat Tvam Asi (The Universal Message in The Bhagavadgita) - Motilal Banarsidas, Delhi,110 007, India- 2:16 and 2:20.

Swami Prabhupada (1985)- The Bhagavadgita (As it is) – Bhaktivedanta Book Book Trust, Watford, Herts, WD2 4XA, UK- 13:1.

Swami Ramsukhdas (2005)- Shrimad Bhagavadgita (Sadhaka Sanjivini)- Gita Press, Gorakhpur, 273 005, UP, India-13:1, 2:16 and 2:20.

Swami Dayananda Saraswati (2006) – Bhagavadgita (Home Study Course) -Sruti Seva Trust, Arsha Vidya Gurukulum, Coimbatore, 641 108, India-13:12:16 and 2:28.

Bibliography
Swami Lokeswarananda (2005)- Shetashvatara Upanisad – Ramakrishna Mission Institute of Culture, Kolkata, 700 029, India-1:9.

3) Human Birth

The goal of life

The goal of life for the jiva (embodied living being), is to detach himself/herself from the false perception, that he /she is the body-mind-intellect complex (ksetram) and rediscover, his/her real nature i.e. he/she is Aatma (the Self/Soul), that ayam (this) Aatma (Self/Soul) Brahma (The Lord)- This Aatma (Self/Soul) is Brahman (The Lord).

Outcome of rediscovering one's real nature

The result of rediscovering one's real nature is that the. spiritual aspirant (sadhaka) sees himself/herself as Aatma (The Self/ soul). He/she sees the same Aatma (Self/ soul) in everyone and everything. Such a person has gone beyond race, religion and country and becomes, a God man on this earth.

Human birth is difficult to obtain

The following extracts emphasizes that human birth is rare: i) "Human birth, desire for liberation and the company of the holy - these three are very difficult to gain in this world. One may get them only by the grace of God".

Bhaja Govindam Chapter 10, p113

ii) Among various living creatures on this earth (jantunam) taking birth (janma) as a human being (nara) is difficult to obtain (durlabham).

Vivekacudamani V2, P7

References

Krishnamani M. N, (1996) - Aadi Shankara's Bhaja Govindam - Dr K. K. Mishra, Rashtriya Sanskrit Sansthan, New Delhi, 110 027, India- Chapter 10 P113.New Delhi, 110 027, India.

Swami Lokeswarananda (2009) - Kathopanisad - Ramakrishna Mission Institute of Culture, Kolkata, 700 029, India- 2:3:4:P 162-163.

Swami Dayananda Saraswati (1997) - Vivekacudamani (Talks on 108 Selected Verses- Sri Gangadhareshwar Trust, Rishikesh, 249 201, India - Verse 2 P113.

4) Death

What is Death?

Death is the withdrawal of the individual Self (jivatman) from the gross (sthula) body (sharira). The individual Self (jivatman) continues and is one with The Lord (ParamAatma), but because of ignorance (avidya) due to attachment to the body/mind/intellect complex (ksetram), it has forgotten its real nature i.e. the Aatma (Self/Soul) and it (Aatma -Self/Soul) and ParamAatma (The Lord) are one and the same.

What happens at death?

Gita 2:22 gives a powerful insight as to what happens when death occurs:

Vaasaamsi jirnaani yathaa vihaaya, navaani grhnaati narah aparaani;
Tathaa shareeraani vihaaya jeernaani, anyaani samyaati navaani dehi.

Vasamsi (garments) jirnani (old and wornout) yatha (just as) vihaya (giving up), navani (new garments) ghrnati (does accept) narah (a man) aparani (others);
tathaa (in the same way) shariraani (bodies) vihaya (giving up) jirnany (old and useless), anyaani (different) samyaati (verily accepts) navaani (new) dehi (the indwller of the body).

<u>Translation</u>

Just as a person gets rid of worn out clothing and wears a new one, similarly, the indweller of the body (Self/Soul) gives up old and worn out bodies and takes on new one.

How to prepare for death

Gita 8 5 gives useful examples on how to prepare for death

i) Anta-kaale ca maam eva, smaran muktva kalevaram;

Yah prayaati sa mat-bhaavam, yati na asti atra samshayah

 Anta (at the end) kale (time) ca (and) mam (me) eva (alone),
 smaran (remembering) muktva (leaving) kalevaram (the body:
 yah (he who) prayaati (departs) sah (he) mad (my) bhavam (nature), yaati (gains) nasty (there is) yatra (here) samshaya (doubt).

<u>Translation</u>

At the time of death, one who departs this body remembering me, he achieves my nature i.e. he is one with me; there is no doubt.

<u>Additional translation</u>

Since our minds accumulate imprints (vasanas) throughout our lives, knowing that we will carry these with us till our death and they will determine our future,

143

in order to gain liberation (moksha), the practice of remembering The Lord from childhood is necessary so that it becomes second nature.

ii) Gita 8:14 says:

Ananya-cetaah satatam, yah maam smarati nityashah;

Tasyaaham sulabhah partha, nitya-yuktasya yoginah.

Ananya-cetaah (with a focusse mind) satatam (always/constantly), yah (the one who) maam (me) smarati (remembers) nityashah (regularly); tasya (to him) aham (I am) sulabhah (easilty gained) partha (O son of Prtha), nitya (regularly) yuktasya (engaged) yoginah (one whose mind is always tranquil).

Translation

The one whose mind, is regularly focused on me and always remembers me, for that one whose mind is tranquil and who is always united with me, I am easy to obtain.

iii) Gita 8:13 and chanting of Om

Om iti eka aksaram brahma, vyaaharan maam anusmaram;

yah prayati tyajan dehaam, sah yaati paramaam gatim.

Om (is The Lord with name and form) iti (thus) eka (the one) aksaram (syllable) Brahma (The absolute Lord), vyharan (vibrating) mam (me) anusmaran (remembering);

yah (the one) prayati (who departs) tyajan (giving up) deham (the body), sah (he) yaati(achieves) paramam (the supreme) gatim (abode).

Translation

One who remembers me on quitting the body, by chanting the one syllabled Om (The name of The Lord with form), attains the most exhalted abode or destination.

iv) Gita 8:7 and the practice of remembering

Tasmaat sarvesu kaalesu, maam anusmara yudhya ca;

mayi arpita-manah buddhi, maam evaesyasi asamshayah

Tasmat (therefore) sarvesu (at all) kaalesu (times), Mam (me) anusmara (go on remembering) yudhya (activities) ca (and);
mayi (unto me) arpita (surrendering) manah (the mind) buddhi (the intellect), mam (unto me) eva (certainly) esyasi (you will gain) asamshaya (there is no doubt).

Translation

Therefore, go on remembering me at all times, surrendering your mind, intellect and activities to me; you will certainly attain me without doubt.

Signs of death

When a person is dying, there is a gradual withdrawal of functions of the organs within the body.

During this life, the senses which are extraverted, act in a manner which is designed, to reap the fruits (phalas) sown in a previous existence (prarabdha karma). When the purpose for which this current bodily existence, came into being is achieved, there is no work for the senses thus they withdraw into the mind.

- **Speech** - there is loss of power of speech because, it merges into the mind. the dying person can think but cannot see or speak.

- **Mind -** this is still alert but, it eventually merges into the life force (prana) then, it ceases to function.

- **Respiration -** though this is taking place, after awhile, it merges into the heat of the body.

- **Body heat** -as long as the person is alive, there is heat.

- **Departure of heat -** when heat leaves, the body slowly becomes cold.

  Everything now merges into the Supreme Self (Sat) then, **Death is said to have occurred.**

Two pursued paths after death

i) The path of no return (Gita 8:24)

Agnir jyotir ahah shuklah, san-maasa uttaraayam;

tatra prayaata gacchanti, brahma brahma-vidah janaah.

Agnir (the God of fire or time) jyoti (God of time or light)
ahah (day) suklah (God of the fortnight of the bright half
of the moon), san (six) maasaah (months) uttara narayana
(The God of the sun's northward journey):
tatra (there) prayaataah (those who die) gacchanti (go),
Brahma (to the absolute) Brahma vidah (who know the
absolute) janah (the people).

Translation

Those who know The Supreme Lord, attains Him by
exiting this world at death, during the influence of the God
of fire or time, God of time and light, God of the day, God
of the fortnight or bright half of the moon and God of the
six months of the sun's travel towards the north.

Additional Translation

The path of no return, is a beautiful and bright route; It's
brightness is due to being illumined by the demigods
(devatas), who are present on this route.

Those who pass along the bright path, first go to the
domain of the fire God (Agni), where they are warmly
welcomed. Then the fire God (Agni) hands them over to
the God of time (Jyoti) who hands them over to the God
of day (Ahah), The God of day (Ahah) hands them over to

the God of the fortnight of the bright half of the moon (Shukla), He in return hands them over to the God of the sun's northward journey (Uttara Narayana) who hands them over to the God of the abode of Brahma (The Supreme Lord). Here, they are liberated, never to return, to the cycle of birth and death (samsara).

ii) The path of return to the cycle of birth and death (Gita 8:25)

Dhoomah ratris tathaa krsnah, san-maasa daksinayanam;

Tatra candaramasam jyotir, yogi praapya nivartate.

Dhoomah (the presiding diety of smoke) ratri (diety of night) tatha (also, similarly) krsna (the diety of the dark fortnight), sat (six) maasaah (months) daksinaayanam (diety of when the sun is travelling south);
tatra (there) chandramasam (planet of the moon) jyotir (light) yogi (the mystic meditator) prapaya (gained or achieved) nivartate (comes back or returns).

Translation

The mystic or the meditator, who passes from this world, travels the path presided over by the Gods of smoke, the night, dark fortnight and the six months when the sun is travelling south; having reached the planet of the moon, returns to the cycle of birth and death (samsara).

<u>Additional translation</u>

Those who traverse the path of return walk on the smoky (dhooma) path (marg). The demigods (devatas) on this path (marg) are administrators of things that represents darkness.

Walking this path, they are met by the god of smoke (dhooma), who hands them over to the god of night (ratri), who in turn hands them over to the god of dark fortnight (krsna), who hands them over to the god of of the six months when the sun is in the southern direction (daksinaayam) who in turn, hands them over to the world of the moon.

Here, they enjoy the fruits of their karmas and once these are exhausted, they return to this world.

Death and the Gunas

<u>Definition of Guna</u>
Guna refers to the quality of mind

<u>The qualities of the mind are</u>

Sattva	-	Purity
	-	Goodness
	-	Knowledge
	-	Illumination

Gita 14:6

Rajas	-	Activity
	-	Passion
	-	Desire
	-	Lust

	-	Selfishness
		Gita 14:7
Tamas	-	Ignorance of what has to be done
	-	Laziness
	-	Apathy
		Gita 14:8

i) Death in Sattva

Gita 14:18 tells us the fate of those who die in Sattva

Urdhavam gacchanti sattvastha

Urdhvam (Higher or upward) gacchanti (go) sattvasthaa (those situated in the mode of goodness)

Translation

Those who are situated in the mode of goodness go to the higher planets

Gita 14:14 qualifies the above statement and adds to it in this manner:

When the jiva (embodied living being) exits this world), in Sattva (mode of goodness), he /she attains the world of those who are pious. This achievement is made possible by the practice of:

• Brahmacarya (Self control)

• Vrat (fasting)

• Danam (being charitable to those in need)

150

- Niskama karma (provision of selfless service to the deserving)

Additional Translation

Those in the mode of Sattva (goodness, purity and knowledge) are reborn, in an environment, where they are given a body/mind/complex (ksetram) to continue their spiritual growth.

ii) Death in Rajas

Rajas is that quality of mind that is characterized by activity, restlessness and desire to acquire.

Gita 14:18 gives this information of their fate:

Madhye tishtanti rajasah

Madhye (in the middle) tishtanti (remain) rajasah (those belonging to rajas).

Translation

Those who are in the rajas (activity, restlessness and desire to acquire) remain in the middle i.e. this earthly plane.

Additional translation

They take birth in homes of those who are engaged in similar pursuits.

Gita 14:15

151

iii) Death in Tamas

Tamas is that quality of mind characterized by ignorance, laziness and apathy. Fate of those who die in Tamas is now revealed by Gita 14:18

Jaghanya guna vrtti-sthaa, adho gacchanti tamasaah.

Jaghanya (of abominable) guna (quality of the mind) vrtti-sthaah (whose occupation), adhah (down) gacchanti (go) tamasah) persons in the mode of ignorance).

Translation

Those who are in Tamas (mode of ignorance, laziness and apathy) are degraded to the world of the hellish. Gita 14:15 says that they are born as bird, beasts, reptiles insects etc.

References

Swami Lokeswarananda (2005) - Chandogya Upanisad-Ramakrishna Mission of Culture, Kolkata, 700 029, India- 6:10:1, 6:11:2, 6:8:6: P 539 and 8:6:5.

Nath P. V. (2002) - Tat Tvam Asi (The Universal Message in The Bhagavadgita) - Motilal Banarsidas, Delhi, 100 007, India-2:22, 8:5:14;13:7, 8:24-25, 14:6-8 and 15.

Swami Prabhupada (1985) - The Bhagavad (As it is) – Bhaktivedanta Book Trust, Watford, Herts, WD2 4XA, UK- 2:22, 14;6-8:18:15.

Swami Ramsukhdas (2005) - Shrimad Bhagavad Gita (Sadhaka Sanjivini) -Gita Press, Gorakhpur, UP, 273 005, India-8:24-25.

Swami Dayananda Saraswati (2007) - Bhagavad Gita (Home Study Course) - Arsha Vidya Gurukulum, Coimbatore 641 108, India- 2:22, 8:5,14, 13,7. 14:6,7,8,18,15.

11

Lifestyles or Pathways to Experience One's Real Nature-Aatma (Self/Soul)

What is our real nature?

Our real nature is that we are Aatma (Self/ Soul) and, Param (The Supreme) atma (Lord) are one and the same and it is:

- Samagram (absolute) Sat (Existence).

- Samagram (absolute) Cit (Consciousness/Awareness).

- Samagram (absolute) Anandam (Bliss).

The Lifestyles or Pathways which enables us to experience our real nature are:

1. **Karma Yoga**

2. **Bhakti Yoga**

3. **Jnana Yoga**

4. **Dhyana Yoga**

Diagram of lifestyles or pathways which enables us to experience our real nature

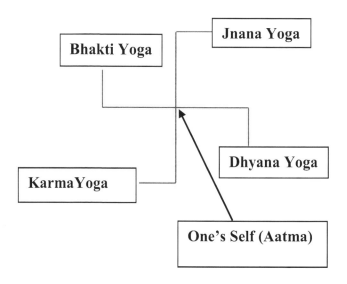

i) Lifestyles or pathways which enables us to experience our real nature - Karma Yoga

What is Karma?

Karma refers to actions of the mind (antah-karana), speech, (vak) and the body (kriya). Swami Harshananda (1995) sees karma (actions) as being restricted to rites and rituals prescribed by the shastras (scriptures). Karma (action) is also viewed as **you reap what you sow.**

What is Yoga

Nath (2002) suggests that yoga is **skill in action in which one utilizes one's intellect (buddhi).** Gita 2:48 says that **evenness of mind** (samatvam) **is called** (ucyate) **yoga.** Other authors inform us that **any work done as an offering to The Lord** (Ishvar-arpana-buddhaya) **is yoga.** Swami Harshananda (1995) sees yoga as **the union of the individual soul** (jivatma) **and The Supreme** (Param) **Soul** (atma).

What is Karma Yoga (The discipline of action)?

Karma Yoga is the performance of selfless service (niskama karma), in which the performer renounces the rewards of his/her efforts (karma-phala tyaga) and, dedicating the work or service along with the rewards to the Supreme Lord (Vishnu-arpam-astu), for the purpose of gaining purity of mind (antah-karana shuddhi) so that, it (the mind) becomes fertile to receive knowledge (vidya) of The Self/Soul (Aatma).

Purpose of Karma Yoga (The discipline of action)

The purpose of Karma (action) Yoga (work done as an offering to The Lord) are:

i) To prepare the mind (antah-karana) to be receptive to Self (Aatma) knowledge (vidya).

Gita 2: 48; p:303.

156

ii) The discharge of one's duties, in order to promote the health and welfare of others in an unselfish manner.

Gita2:3: p131.

iii) To protect one from the great fear (mahata bhayat) of the cycle of birth and death (samsara).

Gita 2:40.

Some examples of Karma Yoga (The discipline of action) **are:**

Actions to promote the health and welfare of one's:

- Parents
- Siblings
- Family members
- Local community
- Region
- Country
- The world
- All members of God's creation

Who are ideal candidates for the Karma Yoga (the discipline of action)?

Karma (action) Yoga (discipline of) is appropriate for those, whose desires (kamas) propel them towards action.

People of this nature are restless and are on the go all the time.

Swami Ramsukhdas (2005) sees householders as being ideal candidates for Karma (action) Yoga (discipline of) as, they provide for the welfare of others. **The ideal way to perform Karma (action) Yoga (the discipline of)**

Gita 3:9 provides the following guidance:

Yajna-arthaat karmano anyatra, loko ayam karma bandhanah;

 Tat-artham karma kaunteya, mukta-sangah samaacara.

Yajna-arthat (performed for the sake of sacrifice) karmanah (than work) anyatra (otherwise), lokah (world) ayam (this person) karma work) bandhanah (bondage or bound):
tat (of him) artham (for the sake) karma (action) Kaunteya (oh! Son of Kunti), mukta (free or liberated) sangah (attachment) samacara (perform perfectly).

Translation

Work done for the sake of yajna (sacrifice) i.e. for Param (Supreme) Aatma (Lord) is liberating otherwise, work binds one to the cycle of births and deaths (samsara). Therefore, O son of Kunti, perform karma (action) without attachment i.e. for The Supreme (Param) Lord (Aatma).

Additional translation

Yajna (sacrifice) includes danam (charity), tapas (austerity), homa (offerings into the sacrificial fire), yatra (pilgrimage to the holy sites) vrat (fasting), study of the shastras (scriptures), Dharma (virtuous conduct), imparting spiritual knowledge and promoting the comfort and welfare of all God's creation.

All karmas (actions) should be carried out with the attitude na (not) mama (mine), i.e. nothing is mine.

Gita 18:9 further adds that all actions, must be enthusiastically and efficiently carried out, without any trace of selfishness, mineness, attachment, desire for rewards, impartially and, in accordance with guidance from the shastras (scriptures).

Why we perform action (karma)

We perform action (karma) for the following reasons:

i) To satisfy our desires

Action (karma) is performed to satisfy a desire (kama). Each one of us have countless desires (kamas), which form imprints (vasanas) in our minds.

ii) To carry out our activities of living

Actions (karmas) enables us to achieve our hygiene, grooming, nutritional, hydrational, excretional, working and recreational needs.

iii) <u>To achieve limited results</u>

Most people act in order to gain limited results such as:

- Wordly (Laukika Karma) results

- Religious outcomes (vaidik karma)

Four types of karmas which influence our lives

Our lives are influenced by four types of Karmas (actions). These are:

i) Sanchita (accumulated) Karma (action).

ii) Prarabdha (ripe or ready to be reaped) Karma (action).

iii) Agami (future) Karma (action).

iv) Kriyamani (instant) Karma (action).

i) Sanchita (accumulated) karma (action)

Sanchita (accumulated) karma (action) is the stored karmas (actions), from all of one's previous lives. It is perceived as one's cosmic debt, because it is saved in the account of the jiva (embodied living being) and, it is to fructify or bear fruits in time to come.

Our dharmic (virtuous) conduct and adharmic (non-virtuous) conduct of our past, are stored or accumulated, to bear fruits in future; hence the saying **you reap what you sow.**

ii) Prarabdha (ripe or fructify) karma (action)

Prarabdha is defined as **that which has begun to give its fruits.** It is part of one's sanchita (accumulated) karma (action) being exhausted in this current existence or life.

Harshananda (1995).

Each birth is determined by the the karma (action) stored in sanchita (accumulated) karma (action) which is ready to bear fruit: this determines suitable parentage and environment to commence working out a portion of the past.

Gita 5:12 p 626

iii) Agami (future) karma (action)

Agami (future) karma (action) refers to karmas (actions) performed during this current existence. This is added to the stored sanchita (accumulated) karma (action) account of the individual and, will bear fruits in time to come i.e. in a future existence.

iv) Kriyamani (instant) Karma (action)

In the course of this existence, some instant karmas (actions) create or incur a cost, which has to be paid in the here and now e.g.

- Paying a speeding fine.

- Serving time in prison for theft.

Karmas (actions) that can and cannot be done

Our shastras (scriptures) advises us about karmas (actions) that can be done and not done.

i) Karmas (actions) that can be done

These Karmas (actions) are:

a) Kamya (desire) Karmas (actions)

Kamya (desire) Karmas (actions) are performed to gain a particular outcome eg:

- Birth of a child.
- Gain employment.
- Pass an educational exam.
- Overcome physical and psychological obstacles in life.

Nath (2002).

b) Nitya (eternal) Karmas (actions)

This refers to daily rituals, such as the carrying out of one's activities of daily living, examples of which are:

- Hygiene.
- Grooming.
- Nutrition.
- Hydration.
- Working.
- Socialization.
- Excretion.

Gita: 3:8

c) Naimittika (occasional) Karmas (actions)

These are Karmas (actions) which are performed, on particular occasions eg:

- Birth of a child.
- Death of a family member.
- Yearly observance of death of a family member (shraddha).
- Marriage ceremony.
- Birthday celebration.

Gita 2:48: P 348

ii) <u>Karmas (actions) that cannot be done (nisiddha)</u>

Nissiddha (forbidden or prohibited) Karmas (actions) should not be done, because they make the mind (antah-karana) impure (ashuddhi) thus, it (the mind) is unfit for spiritual growth.

Swami Harshananda (1995).

Gita 3:8 and 4:17 provide some examples of nisiddha (forbidden or prohibited) Karmas (actions): these are:

- Theft.
- Murder.
- Rape.
- Telling lies.

How to repay our cosmic debt

Definition of our cosmic debt

Our cosmic debt refers to sanchita (accumulated) karmas (actions), from all of our previous lives and which are stored, until the time comes for them to bear fruits i.e. **to reap what we sow.**

Examples of cosmic debt reduction

i) Worship God

We are duty bound to remember our God in thoughts (manasa), speech (vak) and action (karma) thus:

- Our eyes should see Him (The Lord) in everyone and everything we look at.

- Our Ears should hear His transcendental glories and past times in all sound.

- Each breath should remind us that we the Aatma (Soul/Self) and Param (Supreme) Aatma (The Lord) are one and the same.

- Our words should glorify our Lord by being satyam (truthful), shivam (auspicious), sundaram (beautiful), madhuram (sweet), anandam (blissful).

- Our body should be utilized, to serve all our brothers and sisters of creation as The Lord because we are all His eternal fragments (amsha).

Gita 3:8, 3:9

ii) Give thanks to our Saints (Rishis)

We must give thanks to our Saints (Rishis), for being
such wonderful role models and, whose actions are
guided by the religious books (shastras) for the welfare
of all creations.

Gita 3:8, 3:21p122.

iii) Discharge our duties to

a) Our family

We have a duty to unselfishly love, honour and respect our
parents and grandparents, who have laid the foundation
stone, for us to maximise our lives in a positive and
productive manner.

Gita 3:8 and 3:13: p122

b) Duty to our country (Desha) and the world (loka)

Our body/mind/intellect (ksetram) came from the mother
earth, it belongs to mother earth and it will return to
mother earth at death. We should therefore utilize it to
promote the health and welfare of all of our Lord's
creation, by actively collaborating with like-minded
individuals, to serve all (sarva) for the welfare of the world
(loka samgraha).

Gita 3:8

References

Swami Harshananda (1995) - A Dictionary Of advaita Vedanta - Ramakrishna Mat Bangalore, 560 019, India.

Nath P. V (2002)   - Tat Tvam Asi (The Message in The Bhagavad Gita) –Motilal Banarsidas, Delhi, 100 007, India-2:48, 2:40, 3:9, 18:9, 3:13; P 122.

Swami Prabhupada (1985) - Bhagavadgita (As it is) – Bhaktivedanta Book Trust, Watford, WD2 4XA, Herts, UK-3:9 and 18:9.

Swami Ramsukhdas (2005) - Srimad Bhagavadgita (Sadhaka Sanjivini) - Gita Press, Gorakhpur, 273 005, UP, India- 2:3:1: P148, 4:1: P 441, 3:9, 18:9, 5:12: P 626, 3:8, 4:17.

Swami Dayananda Saraswati (2006) - Bhagavadgita – (Home Study Course)- Arsha Vidya, Gurukulum, Coimbatore, 641 109, India- 2:48 :P 303,3:9, 18:9, 3:8, 2:48: P 348 and 4:17.

2. Lifestyles or pathways which enables us to experience our real nature - Bhakti Yoga

What is Bhakti?

Nath (2002) sees bhakti as devotion or worship. He goes on to add that it (bhakti) arises from the root **"bhaj"** and means **"adoration or loving devotion"**. He further adds that it also means **"to share, to partake and to enjoy"**.

Narada Bhakti Sutra 2 explains bhakti as:

Sa tu asmin parama prema-rupa.

Sa (that bhakti) tu asmin (towards Him) parama-prema-rupa (of the nature of supreme love).

Translation

Bhakti has been described as supreme love towards The Lord by the devotee (bhakta).

Additional translation

Love is supreme in the sense that, it is quantitative as well as qualitative. We love Him (The Lord) because He is the only object that is worthy of our highest love.

Some Examples of Supreme Love

In Parama (Supreme) bhakti (love) there is total oneness of the lover and the loved. For example, the gopis of Vrndavan would at times act like Sri Krishna because, their minds were completely absorbed in Him.

Sitaji gave up the comforts of palace life, to accompany Sri Rama - her husband (the 7th incarnation of Vishnu) into exile for fourteen years.

Definition of Yoga

Swami Harshnanda (1995) sees yoga as union of the Jivatma (embodied living being) Param (limitless) Aatma (Lord).

Definition of Bhakti Yoga

Swami Sivananda (1995) sees Bhakti (devotion) Yoga (union), as that yoga (union) through which the bhakta (devotee) unites himself/herself with Param (limitless) Eshvar (Aatma).

Definition of a true Bhakta (devotee)

A real bhakta (devotee) feels secure in his/her love for God and, in God's love for him/her. The only pleasure (kama) he /she seeks is loving God, for him/her God is the most virtuous (dharmic).

In Ayodha Kanda of the Ramayana, it is mentioned, that on his (Bharata) way to meet with Sri Rama (his brother) at Chitrakoota, on reaching the king of holy places (tirtha raja prayag), which is located at the holy confluence of the three great rivers - Ganga, Yamuna and Godavari (Triveni) he prays thus: **"I do not desire wealth (artha) because it gives a false sense of security, nor pleasures and comfort (kama), nor merits (punya) that would make heaven available to me nor freedom from**

168

limitations (moksha). **My only desire is that my heart be filled with love for the lotus feet of Sri Rama**.

Who is Ideal for bhakti (devotion) Yoga (discipline of)?

Bhakti (devotion) Yoga (discipline of) is ideal for the sadhaka (the spiritual aspirant) who is emotional and wants to adore the Supreme (Param) Lord (eshvara) with love.

Three kinds of bhaktis (devotion)

There are three kinds of bhaktis (devotion). These are:

1) Saamaanya Bhakti (ordinary devotion).

2) Ekantha Bhakti (devotion in solitude).

3) Ananya bhakti (single point devotion).

1) Saamaanya Bhakti (ordinary devotion)

Saamaaanya Bhakti (ordinary devotion) is made up of nine components. These are:

a) Sravanam (Listening to the transcendental glories and pastimes of The Supreme (Param) Lord (Ishvar)

Listening to the transcendental glories and pastimes of God (Parameshvar), in association with noble souls (satsanga), purifies the mind (antah-karana shuddhi) so

169

that it is receptive to ingestion and digestion of the message.

Maharaja Parakshit is an example of this component. On account of a sage's curse on him, that he was destinesd to die within a week, he listened with total concentration, on Shuka Gosvami's narration of the transcendental glories and pastimes of The Lord (Ishvar). He was liberated from the cycle of birth and death (samsara) at the end of this time.

b) Kirthanam (chanting the name of as well as praising The Lord).

Bhaktas (devotees) express their love for God in words, song and dance. **Narada Muni** is an excellent example of one who pleased The Lord (Parameshvar) with his constant chanting of His (The Lord) transcendental glories and pastimes.

c) Smaranam (Constant remembrance of The Lord's transcendental glories and pastimes)

Smaranam (constant remembrance of the transcendental glories and pastimes of The Lord) aids in purity of the mind. This is best exemplified by **Prahalad Maharaj**, whose shraddha (faith) in The Lord evolved as a result his constant remembering of The Lord.

d) Pada sevanam (worshipping the lotus feet of The Lord and serving Him with thoughts (manasa), words (vak) and action (kayena).

It is said that devoted service to the Lord's lotus feet, is greater than any treasure in this world. **Lakshmi Devi** provided selfless service (niskama-karma) to the lotus feet of The Lord.

e) Vandanam (prostration)

The whole world is an expression of His divinity and knowing, that we are His eternal fragments (amsha), saluting all with folded hands is a mark of the highest bhakti (devotion). **Akrura Maharaj** a devotee of Sri Krishna exemplifies vandanam (prostration).

f) Archanam (Worshipping the Lord)

A very good example of one who excelled at **archanam** (worshipping) with love and affection is **Emperor Prithu**. His worship of The Lord is made up of sixteen components. These components are:

i) Dhyanam (contemplation on The Divine form of The Lord).

ii) Avahanam (invocation) - chanting a suitable prarthna (prayer) in praise of The Lord.

iii) Asanam (offering an elevated seat to The Lord).

iv) Pada sevanam (washing the feet of The Lord).

v) Ardyam (washing the hands of The Lord).

vi) Achmanam (rinsing the mouth of The Lord).

vii) Naivedanam (offering food to The Lord).

viii) Ritu Phalam (offering seasonal fruits to The Lord).

ix) Achmanam (brushing the teeth of The Lord).

x) Snanam (bathing The Lord).

xi) Vastram (dressing of The Lord).

xii) Janeo (offering sacred thread to The Lord).

xiii) Malam (garlanding of The Lord).

xiv) Chandan (placing sandalwood paste on His forehead).

xv) Dhupam (offering a lighted agarbati to The Lord).

xvi) Deepam (offering a lighted diya to the Lord).

g) Dasyam (Service)

Serving Him with love and affection, unselfishly, is the best way of pleasing Him, as we are his amsha (eternal fragments). **Lord Hanuman** served Sri Rama unselfishly (niskama-karma).

h) Sneham (Friendship)

Seeing the lord as a trusted friend, who you can turn to for guidance, is very comforting. **Arjuna** is a good example of sneham (friendship) with Sri Krishna; this sneham (friendship) culminated with The Lord being his (Arjuna) charioteer in the Mahabharat War and aiding in his (Arjuna's) victory.

i) Aatma naivedanam (total self surrender)

172

Aatma naivedanam (total self surrender) is very pleasing to The Lord. One who approaches The Lord in this manner, will have all his needs met by Him (The Lord). **Bali Maharaj** surrendered himself as well as all his earthly possession at the lotus feet of The Lord.

2) Ekantha Bhakti (Devotion in solitude)

In this form of bhakti (devotion), the bhakta (devotee) sincerely believes that The Supreme Lord is residing within him/her. He/she ascribes a form to The Supreme Lord and worships Him (The Supreme Lord) in that perceived form.

3) Ananya Bhakti (Single pointed devotion)

Nath (2002) identifies three stages in ananya bhakti (single pointed devotion). These are:

a) Jnatum (to be known)

In this stage, there is a realization that there is one God and, He is our friend and protector.

b) **Drastum** (to be seen)

The bhakta (devotee) begins to realize, that the supreme Lord is within Himself/herself (antaryami) and that this same God is in all creation. This vision of seeing God within and in others is referred to as **sarupya.**

c) Pravestum (to enter into)

Having realized that the one God is in all, the bhakta (devotee) drops his/her ahamkara (ego-Iness) and is one with God. He/she is now a **Jivanmukta** (He/she is now one who is liberated even while alive).

Hallmark of a Bhakta (devotee)

1) Advestaa - bears no ill will or hatred all members of The Lord's creation, as his/her mind is totally absorbed in The Lord.

2) Maitrah - the bhakta (devotee) is friendly towards all he/she comes into contact regardless of their attitude towards him/her.

3) Karuna - The bhakta (devotee) is compassionate towards all God's creation.

4) Nirmamah - there is no trace of selfishness nor, feeling of me and mine in him/her.

5) Nirahankarah - The bhakta (devotee) is free from egotism thus, he/she is free from the notion of **I, me** and **mine.**

6) Shama - A bhakta (devotee) is even minded in duhka (distress) and sukhah (happiness). He/she accepts the pairs of opposites as grace of The Lord (prasada buddhi).

7) Ksami - The bhakta (devotee) demonstrates forbearance, forgiveness and maintains self composure in unpleasant situations. Gita 12;13.

174

8) Santustah satatam - A bhakta (devotee) is always contented and satisfied with life as it is for him/her.

9) Yogi - He/she is steady in his/her meditation on The Lord.

10) YataAatmaa - His/her Aatma (body/mind/intellect complex) is yataa (mastered).

11) Drdhanishcaya - The bhakta's (devotee) sraddha (faith) in God is drdh (firm) with nishcaya (clear understanding).

12) Mayi (in Me) **arpita** (engaged) **manah** (the mind) **buddhih** (intelligence). The ksetram body/mind/intellect) is constantly engaged in the service of The Lord.

Gita 12;14

13) Anapeksah – The spiritual aspirant's (sadhaka) only pursuit is to gain Aatma (self) vidya (knowledge).

14) Shucih - All thoughts, speech and action are pure.

15) Daksah - One who has achieved the goal of life i.e. Self/Soul (Aatma) and The Supreme (Param) Lord (Aatma) are one and the same.

16) Udaaseena - An enlightened bhakta (devotee) is indifferent to events and circumstances eg he/she is neutral towards a mitra (friend) or Shatru (enemy).

17) Gata -vyathah - the bhakta (devotee) is free from worries and afflictions, because of faith that he/she is The Aatma (soul).

175

18) **Sarva** (all) **arambha** (new actions) **parityagi** (completely given up). A bhakta (devotee) renounces activities which yields material benefits.

Gita 12:16

19) **Na** (not) **hrsyati** (rejoice) - there is no rejoicing when a desirable gain is obtained.

20) **Na** (not) **dvesti** (hostile) - The bhakta (devotee) is not hostile when an undesirable occurrence takes place.

21) **Na** (not) **Shocati** (does grieve) - Recognizing that losses are part of life, he/she accepts these as a part the scheme of life and, does not grieve.

22) **Na (not) kaanksati (desires)** - He/she does not long for what he/she does not have.

23) **Shubha** (auspicious) **ashubha** (inauspicious) **parityagi** (one who completely gives up) - both auspicious and the inauspicious are given up; He/she only accepts what is given by The Lord.

Gita 12:17

24) **Samah** (even minded) **shatrau** (to an enemy) **mitre** (to a friend) - Because a bhakta (devotee) is free from attachment, his/her interaction with an enemy and friend is even minded.

25) Samah (even minded) - Being even minded, he/she is unaffected by the pairs of opposites e.g. heat and cold etc.

26) Sanga (association) **vivarjati** (free from) - He/she is free from attachment of any kind, because there is no emotional dependence, on people or things.

Gita 12:18

27) Tulya (equal) **ninda** (blame) **stutih** (praise) - He/she is unaffected by blame or praise.

28) Mauni (disciplined in speech) - A bhakta (devotee) is thoughtful, disciplined in speech and constantly thinks of God.

29) Santustah (satisfied) **yena** (with) **kenacit** (anything) - being immersed in bhakti (devotion) to The Lord, He/she manages with the bare necessities.

30) Sthirah (firm) **matih** (knowledge) - His knowledge is that the Self/Soul (Aatma) and The Supreme (Param) Lord (Aatma) are one and the same.

Gita 12:19

Reference

Swami Bhuteshnanda (1999) - Narada Bhakti Sutras - Advaita Ashram, 5 Entally Road, Calcutta, 700 004, India - Sutra2.

Hosien T (1991)- Bhagavan Sri Satya Sai (Discourses Volume 3) The Sri Satya Sai Baba Organization, Trinidad, West Indies-Chapt17: P77-79 and 81-82.

Nath P. V. (2002) - Tat Tvam Asi (The Universal Message in The Bhagavadgita)-Motilal Banarsidas, Delhi, 110 007 - 12: P 481, 12: 13,14, 16, 17, 18,19.

Swami Prabhupada (1985) - The Bhagavadgita (As it is) - Bhaktivedanta Book Trust, Watford, WD2 4XA, U. K - 12:13,14,16,17,18,19.

Swami Ramsukhdas (2005) - Srimad Bhagavadgita - (Sadhaka Sanjivini) - Gita Press, Gorakhpur, U. P. 270 005, India -12:13,14,16,17,18,19.

Swami Dayananda Saraswati (2006) - Bhagavadgita (Home Study Course)- Arsh Vidya Gurukulum, Coimbatore, 641 108, Tamil Nadu, India - 12:13,14,16,17,18,19.

Swami Sivananda (1995) - Ananda Gita (The Song of Bliss) -Divine Life Society, PO Shivanandanagar, 249 192, UP, India -Chap 4: P 32.

Swami Tejomayananda (1996) - Bhakti Sudha - C C M T, Mumbai,400 072, India - P12 and P 35-36.

Swami Tejomayananda (2004) - Manasi Bhakti Sutram - C C M T, Mumbai, 400 072, India - P 33-34 and p56.

3. Lifestyles or Pathways to Experience our Real Nature - Jnana Yoga

Definition of Jnana

Harshananda (1995) reveals that the word **jnana** originates from **jna** (to know). He goes on to add that **jna** refers to **intuitive experience.**

Swami Ramsukhdas (2005) sees **jnana** (knowledge) as **vijnana** (real knowledge) because it reveals that this world is a manifestation of Divinity.

To know The Lord (Ishvar) as one's own Self (Aatma/Soul) and to behold or see the Self/Soul (Aatma) in all of The Lord's (Ishvar) creation (srsti) is jnana (knowledge).

Definition of Yoga

According to Swami Harshananda (1995), **yoga** originated from the root **yuj;** it is that which unites The Self/Soul (Aatma) with The Supreme (Param) Lord (Aatma).

Definition of Jnana Yoga

Jnana (knowledge) yoga (that which unites) is the realization, by the acquisition of vidya (knowledge), that The Aatma (Self/Soul) and Param (Supreme) Aatma (Lord) are one and the same and this Aatma (Self/Soul) is in all of The Lord's creation.

Who is best suited to Jnana (Knowledge) Yoga (the discipline of)

Jnana (knowledge) yoga (the discipline of), can be pursued by any Bhakta (devotee) but, it is ideally suited to those individuals, who are introspective by nature and whose analytical skills are fairly well developed and, who wants to go beyond the visible.

Benefits of the acquisition of Jnana (knowledge) Yoga (the discipline of)

Jnanam (Knowledge) yoga (the discipline) pavitram (the greatest purifier). Gita 4:37 and 4:38 validates this statement as follow Yathaa edhaamsi sammiddhah agnir, bhasma-saat kurute arjuna; jnana agnih sarva-karmaani, bhasma-sat kurute tathaa.

Yatha (just as) aidhamsi(firewood) samsiddha (well lighted) agnih(fire), bhasma-sat (ashes) kurute (turn) Arjuna (o Arjuna);
jnana agnih (the fire of knowledge) sarva (all) karmani (actions), bhasma-sat (to ashes) kurute (turns) tatha (so too).

Translation

Just as blazing fire reduces firewood to ashes, similarly, the fire of knowledge, reduces all actions to ashes.

Gita 4:37

Na hi jnaanena sadrsham, pavitram iha vidyate; tat svayam yoga-samsidddhah, kaalena atmani vindati

Na (nothing) hi (therefore) jnaanena (knowledge) sadrsham (in comparison), pavitram (that which purifies) iha (in this world) vidyate (exists);

Tat (that knowledge) svayam (naturally) yoga-samsiddhah (one who has been prepared through karma yoga), Kalena (in time) aatmani (in himself) vindati (gains/enjoys)

Translation

Therefore, in this world, there is no purifier in comparison to knowledge, of The Aatma (Self/Soul) that exists. One who has gained maturity of mind, during the course of time through **karma yoga** (the discipline of selfless action), gains or attains this knowledge.

Gita 4:38

Additional Translation

This maturity of mind can be gained by:

- Yajna (sacrifice).
- Danam (being charitable to the deserving).
- Kirthanam (chanting The Lord's name (s) with prema (love).
- Vrat (fasting).
- Dhyanam (the discipline of meditation).
- Pranayama (breath restraint).

181

- Snanam (bathing in the holy rivers eg Ganga, Yamuna etc.)

Gita:4: 38.

All sins will be overcome by knowledge

Sarvam jnana-plavena eva, vrjinam santarisyasi

Sarvam (all) jnana (knowledge) plavena (raft or boat) eva (alone), Vrjinam (the ocean of sin) santariyasi (you will cross with ease).

Translation

You will cross over all sins with complete with the boat of knowledge.

Gita 4:36

Additional Translation

Karmas (actions) performed in ignorance of the Aatma (Self/Soul) becomes papas (sinful) The same karma (action) performed with full knowledge of The Aatma (Self/Soul) becomes a virtue. Sri Krishna is saying that even the worst sinners can cross the ocean of sin by the boat (plavena) of knowledge. (jnana).

It is to be remembered that this jnana (knowledge) is that we are Aatma (Self/Soul), that ayam (this) Aatma (Self/Soul) Braham (is The Lord).

Gita 4:36:and 5:16

Knowledge of Aatma (Self/Soul) and The Param (Supreme)

Aatma (The Self/Soul) and **ParamAatma** (The infinite Lord) are one and the same; it is uttamam (the most exhalted) and Param (ultimate) Jnanam (knowledge) because it leads to moksha (freedom from limitations).

Gita 14:1: p2

The means for obtaining this jnanam (knowledge) are:

- Shravanam (listening to scriptures/shastras from a competent spiritual master to gain knowledge).

- Mananam (analysis of what has been heard to make sure that it is understood inorder to clear all doubts).

- Nidididhysana (The practice of self enquiry/Aatma vichar by deep and intense contemplation).

Gita 14:2: p 3

The acquisition of Aatma (Self/Soul) vidya (knowledge)is dependent on several factors:

These factors are:

1) Ishvar (The Lord's) Anugraha (grace)

Only by the grace (anugraha) of The Lord (Ishvar) can the spiritual aspirant (sadhaka) be blessed with Aatma

(Self/Soul) vidya (knowledge). This anugraha (grace)can be gained by sarangathi- total surrender of one's self at the lotus feet of The Lord.

2) Demonstrate equality of vision

The bhakta (devotee) should perceive the imperishable (nitya) Supreme (Param) Lord (Aatma) in all members of His creation. The following guidance is provided by
Gita: 6:9:

Suhrn-mitrary-udaasina, madhyastha-dvesya-bandhusu;

Saadhusv api ca paapesu, sama-buddhir vishisyate.

Suhrt (to well-wisher) mitra (friend) ari (enemies) udasina (neutrals), madhyasta (mediators) dvesya (envious) bandhusu (relatives);

Sadhusu (the pious) api (as well as) ca (and) paapesu (sinners), sama (the same) buddhih (whose vision) vishisyate (most exhalted or advanced).

Translation

One who regards a well wisher, a friend, an enemy, a neutral, mediators, the envious, relatives, the pious and sinners with equal vision or equal mindedness, that one, is the most exhalted or advanced.

184

Gita 13:28 adds the following:

Samam sarvesu bhootesu, tisthantam parameshvaram;

Vinashyatsv avinashyantam, yah pashyati sa pashyati.

Samam (the same) sarvesu (in all) bhutesu (living beings), tisthantam (residing) parama (ultimate/limitless) Eeshvaram (The Lord);
Vinashyatsu (in the perishable) avinashyantam (not destroyed),
yah (one who) pashyati (sees) sah (he) pashyati (actually sees).

Translation

One who sees the same imperishable Supreme Lord, residing in all perishable beings equally, he alone sees.

3) A committed mind is needed

Since knowledge (jnanam) takes place in the inner instrument called the mind (antah-karana), it needs to be committed in terms of focus, so that the message can be ingested, digested and assimilated.

Gita 7:1: p 434. makes this point very well:

Mayi asaktamanaah madaashryah maam jnaasyasi

Mayi (in Me) asaktamanah (one whose mind is committed) madashraya (having surrendered to me) mam (Me) jnaasyasi (you will know).

Translation of Gita 7: p:434

One whose mind is committed and surrendered to me will know me.

4 Faith and self control are needed

Gita 4:39 emphasises the need for faith and self control:

Shraddhaavan labhate jnaanam, tat-parah samyata endriyah;

Jnaanam labdhva param shantim, acirena addhigacchati.

Shraddhaavaan (one who has faith in the scripture and the teacher) labhate (gains or achieves) jnanam (knowledge), tat-parah (one who is committed to knowledge) samyata (controlled or mastered) indriyah (the senses);
Jnanam (Knowledge) labdhava (having gained or achieved) Param (absolute) shaantim (peace), acirena (very soon or immediately) adhigacchati (gains or attains).

<u>Translation</u>

One who has faith in the scripture and the teacher, is committed to the pursuit of this knowledge and has control or mastery of the senses, this sadhaka (spiritual aspirant) will, obtain this knowledge.

What the Lord wishes the spiritual aspirant (sadhaka) to know

Our Lord wishes us to know the following:

<u>i) He is the creator of everything</u>

Gita 10:8 is supportive of this statement:

Aham sarvasya prabhavo, mattah sarvam pravartate.

Aham (I am) sarvasya (of all) prabhavah (The Creator), mattah (from Me) sarvam (everything) pravartate (is sustained).

<u>Translation</u>

I am the creator of all and everything is sustained by Me.

<u>Additional Translation</u>

The Lord (Brahman) is the material (upadana) cause (karana) and the efficient (nimitta) cause (karana) of all creation. Everything in this world owe their existence to Him (The Lord Brahman).

Gita 10:8; p1160-1161

ii) The Lord is the highest

This is summed up very nicely in Katha Upanisad 1:3;11:

Purusaan na param kinchit, sa kaastha saa paraa gatih.

Purusaan (The Lord) na (nothing) param (superior) kincit (there is), sa (that) kaastha (the limit of growth) sa (that) param (the highest or Supreme) gatih (goal).

Translation

There is nothing superior or higher than The Lord. That is the end of all growth. He is the highest goal achievable.

iii) The Lord cannot be born

Although the Lord (Ishvara) creates, sustains and dissolves creation, He has no doership (kartrtva) nor enjoyership (bhoktrtva), nor does He receive the results of action (karma phalas) which is the cause of birth therefore, He (The Lord) cannot be born. When it is said that He has descended into this material world, it means that He assumes a body for the purpose of the descent; He does not take himself to be the body.

Gita 4:6: p 31

iv) The Lord is absolute (samagram) existence (Sat)

The Lord is samagram (absolute) Sat (existence) is confirmed by Gita 4:5:

Bahooni me vyateetani, janmaani tava ca arjuna;
Taani aham veda sarvaani, na tvam vettha parantapa

Bahooni (many) Me (for Me) vyateetaani (have passed),
janmaani (births) tava (for you) ca (and) Arjuna (O
Arjuna): Taani (those or them) aham (I) veda (do know)
sarvaani (all), na (not) tvam (you) vettha (know)
Parantapa (O subduer of the enemy).

Translation

O Parantapa you and I have passed through many births;
I know them all whereas, you do not O subduer of
enemies.   Gita 4:5

Additional Translation

The Lord is a yukta yogi ie He knows the past, present
and future of all beings, this is substantiated by Gita
7:26:

Veda aham samateetani, vartamaanaani ca arjuna;

Bhavisyaani ca bhootaani, maam tu veda na kashcana

Veda (know) aham (I) samateetaani (complete past),
vartamaanani (present) ca (and) Arjuna (O Arjuna)
bhavisyaani (future) ca (and) bhutani (all living beings),
mam (Me) tu (but) veda (know) na (not) kashcana (no
one).

189

Translation of Gita 7:26

I know the complete past, present and future of all living beings; I also know all living beings but, no one knows Me.

v) The Lord is the eternal seed in all beings

This is stated in the following verses of Gita as stated below:

a) Gita; 7:10

Beejam maam sarva bhootaanaam

Beejam (the seed) mam (Me - The Lord) sarva (in all) bhootaanam (beings).

Translation
I am the original seed in all living beings.

b) Gita 10:39

Beejam aham sarva bhootaanam

Beejam (seed) aham (I am) sarva (in all) bhootaanam (creation).

Translation

I am the generating seed in all creation.

190

c) Gita 14:4

Aham -beeja-pradah pita

Aham (I am) bija (seed) pradah (giving) pita (father)

Translation

I am the seed giving father.

vi) The Aatma (Soul/Self) is amshah (a fragment of God).

Mama eva amshah jeeva loke, jeeva-bhootah sanaatanah.

Mama (My) amshah (fragment) eva (only) jiva (embodied living being) Loke (world), Jiva (embodied living being) bhutah (being) sanatanah (eternal).

Translation

An eternal fragment of my own self has become the soul in the world of the living.

Gita: 15:7

Additional Translation

The Soul/Self being a fragment of God, abides in Him (God); the body/mind/intellect complex (ksetram) is a fragment of nature (prakrti) and abides in it. Offering the body/mind/intellect complex (ksetram) to the world and, offering the Soul/Self as a gift to God, is freedom from limitation (moksha).

Gita: 15:7: p 1625.

Reference

Harshananda (1995)   - A Dictionary of Advaiti Vedanta - Ramakrishna Math, Bangalore, 560 019, India.

Nath. P. V. (2002)   - Tat Tvam Asi (The Universal Message in The Bhagavad Gita) - Motilal Banarsidas, Delhi,100 007, India - 4:37, 4:38, 4:36: P 167, 5:16, 6:9, 13:27, 4:39, 10:8, 4:6,4:5, 7:26, 7:10,10:39, 14:4, 15:7.

Swami Prabhupada (1985) - The Bhagavadgita (As it is) - Bhaktivedanta Book Trust, Watford, WD2 4XA, U. K -7:2: P 819, 4:37, 4:38, 4:36, 5:16, 6:9,13:27,4:39, 10:8, 4:6, 4:5, 7:26, 7:10, 10:39, 14:4, 15:7.

Swami Ramsukhdas (2005) - Srimad Bhagavadgita (Sadhaka Sanjivini)- Gita Press, Gorakhpur, 270 005, U. P. India -10:8: P 1160-1161, 4:6, 4:5, 7:26, 7:10, 10:39,14:4, 15. 7: P 1625.

Swami Dayananda Saraswati (2006) - Bhagavadgita (Home Study Course)- Arsha Vidya Gurukulum, Coimbatore, 641 108, Tamil Nadu, India -4:37, 4:38, 4:36; P1 14:1: P 2, 14:2: P3, 6:9,7:1:P 434, 13:27, 4:39, 10:8, 4:6: p31, 4:5,7:26, 7:10, 10:39, 14:4, 15:7.

4. Lifestyles or Pathways to Experience Our Real Nature - Dhyana Yoga

Definition of Dhyana

Swami Harshananda (1995) sees dhyana (meditation) as a state in which the mind flows freely and continuously towards the object of contemplation. Dhyansvrupam verse 1 cites dhyana as:

Dhyanam naama svarupasya sahajanbhanam ucyate

Dhyanam (meditation) naama (is the name) svarupasya (of one's true nature) sahajan (effortless) bhanam (awareness) ucyate (is called).

Translation

Effortless awareness of one's true nature is the name given to dhyanam or meditation.

Dhyanam Svarupam Verse 1

Definition of Yoga

According to Swami Harshanada (1995) Yoga is that which unites Aatma (The Self/Soul) with Param (Supreme) Aatma (Lord).

Definition of Dhyana Yoga

Dhyana yoga is the 7th limb of the 8th limb yoga (union) sutra (thread which holds the eight limbs together). It is

193

a process of withdrawing the senses, from the sense objects. by turning them within, so that the body/mind/intellect complex (ksetram), can become calm and relaxed thus making it possible, for a heightened sense of awareness to be experienced.

Two types of Dhyana (meditation)

These are:

i) Dhyana (meditation) - is the focus on God with form (Saguna Brahman) eg Rama, Krishna, Shiva and Ganesh.

ii) Nididhysana (contemplation) - this is the focus on God without form (Nirguna Brahman) e.g. Om.

Who is fit for Dhyana (meditation) Yoga (discipline of)?

Those who possess an introverted personality i.e. those who are at ease being on their own; however, any one with practice over time can be conditioned to this process.

Purpose of Dhyana (meditation)

The purpose of dhyana (meditation) is to gain antah-karana shuddhi (purity of mind) by freeing ourselves from our internal enemies such as;

- Kama (desires for material objects).

- Krodhah (anger).

- Lobha (greed).

- Moha (delusion).

- Matsarya (envy).

- Mada (pride).

- Ragas (attachments).

- Dvesas (hatred/dislikes).

With antah-karana shuddhi (purity of mind), comes the ability to focus on the object of one's Dhyana (meditation).

Gita: 6:10

The Act of Meditation

1) Conditions for meditation

Gita 6:17 provides the following guidance:

Yukta aahara vihaarasya, yukta-cetasya karmasu;

Yukta-svapna-avabodhasya, yogo bhavati duhkha-ha.

Yukta (regulated) aahara (eating) viharasya (recreation), yukta (regulated) cetasya (work for maintenance) karmasu (in discharging duties);

yukta (regulated) svapna (sleep) avabodhasya
(wakefulness);
yoga (meditation) bhavati (becomes) duhkha-ha
(destroyer of sorrow).

Translation of Gita 6:17

He who is moderate in eating, recreation, action, sleep and
wakefulness, yoga becomes the destroyer of sorrows
which originates from the cycle of birth and death
(samsara).

2) Prerequisite for meditation

a) Anugraha (God's grace) is needed

Without God's grace, nothing is possible. Antah-karana
shuddhi (purity of mind) will not take place. His grace
will only descend, if the sadhaka (spiritual aspirant) is
sincere in his /her desire for liberation (moktum iccha),
prays with faith (shraddha) and surrenders completely
(sarangathi) to His (The Lord's) will.

b) Shraddha (Faith)

A faithful person (shraddha-van) who believes, that
he/she is Aatma (Self/Soul), and who knows that this same
Aatma (Self/Soul) is Brahman (The Lord), will find
obstacles to this realization removed by the lord.

c) Aparigraha (Free from feelings of possessiveness)

Hoarding or gathering (parigraha) is a huge problem to spiritual growth, because, it is a barrier to dhyanam (meditation).

d) Nirashih (Freedom from longings) Internal and external pressures, in the form longing for material pleasure and prosperity contaminates the mind thus, it is not available for dhyanam (meditation).

e) Yata (mastery) citta (memories of the past) Aatma (the physical body)

A sadhaka (spirtual aspirant), should aim to keep the ksetram (body/mind/intellect) totally relaxed so that antah-karana (the mind) is quietened, and it is prepared for dhyanam (meditation).

f) Ekaki (alone)

Dhyanam (meditation) is successful, when the striver is alone and free from   distraction from people and noise.

Gita 6:10

g) The Environment for Meditation

The environment can be a:

- Room in your house.

- Quiet corner in your garden.

- Quietness is needed to prevent distraction of the mind.

- Warm and well-ventilated environment to aid comfort and respiration.

- Pleasant atmosphere to create a positive environment.

h) Food and clothing

Consuming a heavy meal, an hour before the practice of dhyanam (meditation), diverts blood from the brain to the stomach to aid digestion, thus, this leads to sleepiness. Wearing of loose fitting clothing, aids free circulation of air to the body thus, maintaing a conducive body temperature which aids successful dhyanam. (Meditation).

i) Setting for Dhyana (meditation)

- Shucau (sanctified/clean) Deshe (place/land) - a clean place is conducive for dhyanam (meditation), as it invigorates and elevates the mind.

- Vivikta (quiet) - a quiet place calms the sense and aids introspection.

j) Asanam (the seat) for Dhyanam (meditation)

- Sthiram (firm) - firmness of the seat, prevents physical movements thus, ensuring concentration is maintained throughout the process of dhyanam (meditation).

- Na (not) ati (too) ucchhrtitam (high) na (not) atinica (too low) - high seats can result in unsteadiness and falls; Low seats can be the cause of physical discomforts.

- The Ideal asanam (seat) for dhyanam (meditation) should be the following:

  - Kusha (grass mat) should be used as the base as it keeps the asanam (seat) warm.

  - Ajina (deer skin) should constitute the middle layer, as it is conducive to peace, tranquillity and aids control over the mind.

  - Caila (soft cloth) is placed over the deerskin to give a sense of comfort.

Gita 6:11-12

k) Physical position and mental composure for dhyana (meditation)

i) Samam kaya shirah grivam, dharayaan acalam stirah.

Samam (straight) kaya (body) shirah (head) grivam (neck), dharayaan (holding) acalam (without moving) stirah (still)

<u>Translation</u>

One should hold one's body, head, and neck still in one straight line with the hands, placed on the knees.

<u>Rationale for this posture</u>

This posture aids in the acquisition of a calm and focussed mind.

Gita 6:13.

ii) Sampreksya nasik agram svan.

Sampreksya (looking at) nasik (nose) agram (the tip) svan (one's own)

<u>Translation</u>

The striver should look at the tip of his/her nose.

Rationale

He/she should look at the tip of his/her nose with half closed eyes, to prevent falling asleep and to reduce visual inputs thus aiding in a strong focus.

Gita 6:13

iii) Sthirah (still)

The striver should sit like a statue, for five (5) minutes each day for seven (7) days and slowly lengthen the time factor, over the coming weeks.

Rationale

This effort will aid in overcoming the strain of the posture and conquering of the posture (jitaasana). It will lead to the mind being withdrawn from the body.

Gita 6:13

l) The best time of the day for Dhyana (meditation)

It is recommended, that the following times of the day, are the most auspicious for dhyanam (meditation) because purity of mind predominates thus, our saints and sages, meditate at these times. These times are:

- 4 am to 6 am. and 12:00 to 1:00pm
- 4. 00 to 5. 00 pm and 6:00 to 8:00 pm

m) Some suggested aids for Dhyana (meditation)

- An altar with your favourite deity.
- A japa mala (rosary),
- A sweet smelling agarbati (joss stick) or a candle.
- A box of match or a cigarette lighter to light the agarbati (joss stick) or candle.

3) The Process of Dhyana (Meditation)

i) Invocation prayer for peace and removal of obstacles to a successful dhyanam (meditation).

Stand behind your seat, which is in front of your altar with eyes closed and folded hands, chant the following prayer, or one of your choice.

Om shuklaam bara dharam vishnum, Shashi varnam chaturbhujam; prassanna vadanam dhaayet sarva vighno upashantaye

Om (The Lord) shuklaambaradharam (one who wears white clothes) vishnum (all pervasive), Shashivarnam (one who is the colour of the moon) chaturbhujam (four armed);
Prasannavadanam (one who has a cheerful face) dhyaatet (may one meditate on), sarva (all) vighna (difficulties) upashantaye (resolution of).

202

<u>Translation of invocatory prayer</u>

I meditate on the all -pervasive Lord, who is clothed in white garments, who is the colour of the moon, who has four arms, and who has a cheerful countenance, for the removal of all obstacles.

Prayer Guide- mantras and Stotras 117.

ii) Mentally consecrate your asana (seat)

Still standing with folded hands and eyes closed, now chant the following mantra (prayer) to spiritualize your asana (seat):

Om prthivi tvaya dhrita loka Devi,
tvam Vishnu dhrita;
tvam cha dhaarya Maa Devi,
pavitram kuru cha asanam.

<u>Translation of this mantra (prayer)</u>

Dear mother earth, the various worlds are borne by you; you are borne by Lord Vishnu. I beseech you to bear me as well and consecrate this seat.

iii) The meditator now sits on his/her sanctified asana (seat)

iv) The meditator now washes his/her hands mentally

Mentally go through the process of washing the hands by chanting the following mantra (prayer).

Om hasta prakshalam samarpayami.

Translation of this mantra (prayer)

Dear Lord, it is my desire that you purify these hands, so that their role in this act of dhyanam (meditation), is pleasing to you.

Rationale for cleansing our hands

- Lakshmiji (Lord of spiritual wealth) resides on our fingers, Saraswatiji (Lord of knowledge) lives on our palms and Govinda (The Lord of creation) abode is on our wrist.

- The hands are symbol of service thus, washing them purifies them for the act of dhyanam (meditation).

v) Antar (internal) shuddhi (purification).

Mentally place a teaspoon of water in your right palm, with the left palm beneath it, and and go through the act of drinking it, while chanting this mantra (prayer) three times:

- **Om Shri Krishna namah** - as I sip this sacred water, I offer my sincerest salutations and surrender to the lotus feet of Shri Krishna (Lord of the world).

- **Om Shri Rama Namah** - as I sip this sacred water, I offer my sincerest salutation and surrender to the lotus feet of Shri Rama (Lord of the world).

- **Om shri Narayana Namah** - as I sip this sacred water, I offer my sincerest salutation and surrender to the lotus feet of Shri Narayana (Lord of the world).

Translation

I pray that Shri Krishna, Shri Rama and Shri Narayana, which are names for the one God, purify my internal organs.

Adapted from Pujaamritam p 10.

Rationale

The internal structures of the body, are actively engaged in making our activities of living possible. Their purity, will increase their longevity so that the meditator can achieve his/her goal in life.

vi) Manasa (mental) Shuddhi (purification) of different parts of the body

The meditator now mentally places a teaspoon of water on his/her left palm; using the ring finger of the right hand, he/she now immerses the ring finger into the mental water in the left palm and touches the following parts of the body, as the following mantras (prayers) are chanted:

- **Om bhuh punatu shirashi** - Let the region of bhuh purifies our head, so tha it is fit for Aatma (Self /Soul) vidya (Knowledge).

- **Om bhuvah punatu netrayoh** - Let the region of bhuvah purifies our eyes, so that they see The Lord in everyone and everything they look at.

- **Om svah punatu kanthe** - Let the region of svah purify our throat, so that our speech is truthful (satyam), loving (priyam) and for the welfare of the world (hitam).

- **Om maha punatu hridaye** - Let the region of maha purify our hearts, so that the flowers of our heart are are in perpetual bloom, ensuring that their soft petals are always available, to embellish the lord's lotus feet as well as for garlanding Him with our love and affection.

- **Om janah punatu naabhyam** - Let the region of janah purifiy our abdominal region, so that it always acts as our moral and ethical compass ensuring that each performed action (karma), is in the mode of goodness (sattva)

- **Om tapah punatu padyoh**- Let the region of tapah, purify our legs, so that they have the strength to take this mandir of The Lord, wherever He wishes it to go.

- **Om satyam punatu shirasi** - Let this region purifies our head so that it is always fit for Aatma (Self/Soul) vidya (knowledge).

- **Om kham Brahma punatu sarvatra** - May the Creator (Brahma) purify this entire body so that it is fit to serve the Lord and the world.

Adapted from Hindutvam p3

vii) Prana (breathing) **yama** (restraint or control of)

a) Puruka (inhalation)

- Close the right nostril by sealing it with the thumb of right hand.

- Exhale through the left nostril.

- Now inhale to the count of five (5).

- As you inhale, say mentally to yourself **aham Brahmasmi** (I am The Lord)

b) Kumbhaka (Retention of breath)

- Now seal the left nostril with the ring finger of the right hand.

- Hold the breath for a count ten (10).

- During this retention mentally say to yourself **aham Brahmasmi** (I am The Lord).

c) Recaka (exhalation)

- Now remove the thumb of the right hand from right nostril and exhale to a count of five (5).

- As you exhale, mentally say to your self **aham Brahmasmi** (I am The Lord).

N.B. Recaka (breathing out), puraka (breathing in) kumbhka (holding the breath) and recaka (exhalation) constitutes one round of pranayama (breath control).

Benefits of Prana (breath) Yama (control of)

- It makes the respiratory system more efficient thus, more oxygen is available to carry out one's activities of living.

- It has a calming effect on the mind and aids clarity of thinking.

Adapted from Yoga, Mind and Body. P113.

viii) Focus on meditation

a) Open eyes method

The meditator could focus on:

- Smell of a lighted agarbati (joss stick).

- Flame of a lighted candle.

- Focus on your favourite diety.

b) Half eyes closed method

- Can focus on the tip of the nose.

c) Fully closed eyes method

- Visualization of one's favourite diety.

ix) The act of Dhyanam (meditation)

- **Asana** - sit in your preferred place of meditation.

- **Conducive environment** - clean, warm, well ventilated.

- **Clothing** - loose fitting and comfortable.

- **Asana** - sit on a seat that is comfortable.

- **Position of the body** - head, neck and body in a straight line.

209

- **Focus on meditation** - open, half closed or completely closed.

- **Japa mala (prayer beads)**

   - Hold it in your right hand.

   - Rest string between the the first bead.

   - Use thumb of the right hand to move each bead to the chant of your chosen mantra (prayer) in a clockwise direction.

   - When you reach the end of end of the last bead (the beads are 108 in total) you stop. This constitute one round of dhyanam (meditation).

   - When you reach the last bead, do not cros over to the meru (the bead which anchors the strings that hold all the beads together.).

   - Your mantra (prayer) could be on your chosen deity eg Om Shri Rama Namah - my prostration, salutation and surrender to the lotus feet of The Lord or a mantra of your own.

x) Conclusion of the Act of Dhyana (meditation)

A mantra (prayer) of your choice or, this mantra (prayer)
is a good way of conclusion.

Om kayena vaachaa manas indriyairvaa,
buddhya aatma naavaa prakrite svabhaa vaat,
karomi yadyat sakalam parasmi,
Naarayaneti samarpayami

Translation

Whatever I perform with this ksetram
(body/mind/intellect) intentionally or otherwise, I
dedicate all this, to the Lotus feet of The Param
(Supreme) Aatma (Lord).

xi) Thank God for the opportunity for this Dhyanam
(meditation).

In quiet contemplation, thank God for the opportunity for
this satsang (association with Him). Beseech Him with
request to have more satsangas (association with Him).

**xii) Now you can get up from your asana (seat) and
recommence your activities of living.**

Benefits of Dhyana (meditation) **Yoga** (the discipline of)

i) Physiological

- Musculo/skeletal system, becomes more effective in it's ability, to carryout one's activities of living.

- Energy Levels - increased.

- Respiratory System - more efficient respiration.

- Heart - lower risk of cardiovascular disease.

- Immune System - stronger and better able to defend the body against infections.

- Cerebral - improved academic performance, improved decision making and enhanced creativity.

- Ageing - slows down the ageing process therefore, increases longevity.

- Weight loss - have been known to promote weight loss.

ii) Psychological

- Promotes self confidence.
- Strengthens focus and concentration.

212

- Improves memory.
- Aids in the development of peace of mind, calmness and emotional maturity.
- Leads to the development of a strong will power.

3) Spiritual

- Sees the same Self/Soul (Aatma) in all of God's creation.
- More compassionate and caring.

(These benefits have been culled from a variety of sources).

Reference
Swami Harshananda (1995) - A Dictionary of Advaita Vedanta- Ramakrishna Math, Bangalore, 560 019, India.

Kindersley D.   (1998) - Yoga, Mind and Body -Dorling Kindersley,80 Strand, London, WC2 ORL, UK – P:113.

Nath P. V. (2002) - Tat Tvam Asi (The Universal Message in The Bhagavadgita) - Motilal Banarsidas, Delhi, 110 007,
India - 6:17, 6:10, 6:11-12, 6:13.

Swami Prabhupada (1985) - The Bhagavadgita (As it is) - Bhaktivedanta Book Trust Watford, WD2 4XA, Herts, U. K - 6:10, 6:11-12, 6:13.

Swami Purnananda (1980) - Aum Hindutvam (Vedic Prayer – Hindu Catechism) - Swami Purnanda, London, W12, UK – P:3.

Ramdas. K (1995) - Pujamritam (The Nectar of Worship) - Ramdas, Trinidad, West Indies – P 10 and 21.

Swami Ramsukhdas (2005) -Srimad Bhagavadgita (Sadhaka Sanjivini) - Gita Press, Gorakhpur, 270 005, UP, India- 6:17, 6:10, 6:11-12, 6:13.

Swami Dayananda Saraswati (2006) - Bhagavad Gita (Home Study Course) - Arsha Vidya Gurukulum, Coimbatore, 641 108, Tamil Nadu, India - 6:11-12: p306-308, 6:17, 6:10.

Swami Dayananda Saraswati (2005) - Prayer Guide - Arsha Vidya Gurukulum, Saylorsburg, Pennsylvania, PA 18353, USA – P:117.

12

The Human Mind and its role in Liberation (Moksha)

What is the Mind?

Swami Tejomayananda (2010) sees the mind, as **a continuous flow of thoughts** whereas, Swami Lokeswarananda (2010) perceives it **as the controller of the senses;** he goes on to add, that it (the mind), is the daivam (divine) chaksu (eyes) because, the Aatma (Self/Soul) sees through it.

Functional Composition of the Mind

The mind is referred to as:

a) Antah (that which abides within) Karana (the means of knowledge).

Translation

That which abides within and is the means via which knowledge is gained.

Functional composition of the Mind

i) **Manas** (Mind) - is engaged in the process of decision making; it receives information from the senses. It is emotional and indecisive.

ii) **Buddhi** (Intellect) - makes rational decision based on analysis of incoming information.

iii) **Cittam** (will or memory) - houses information which are needed, to aid in the carrying out one's activities of living.

iv) **Ahamkara** (Ego) - When the manas (mind) sees itself as part of sharira (the body), it is called ahamkara (**ego**); The ahamkara (**ego**) is seen as the personality of the individual,

Our Mind is like a Battlefield where Opposing Thoughts Battle it out

Our manas (minds) are inhabited with both good and bad thoughts; bad thoughts will lead to a down ward spiral and eventual degradation. Good thoughts will lift us up and remind us of our Divine inheritance i.e. we are the Aatma (Self/Soul), that Param (Supreme) Aatma (Lord) and the Aatma(Self/Soul) are one and the same thus, we are eternal.

216

There is a constant battle for dominance, between the forces of dharma (good or virtuous conduct) and the force of adharma (evil/bad or sinful conduct) in our manas (minds). Since we are on a pilgrimage to experiencing our real nature which is Divinity, Gita 6: 5 provides the following advice:

Uddhared aatmana aatmaanam, na atmaanam avasaadayet;

aatma eva hy aatmano bandhur, aatma eva ripur aatmanah.

Uddharet (may one lift) aatmanah (one self) aatmaanam (by oneself), na (not) aatmaanam (one self) avasaadayet (may one destroy);
aatma (one self) eva (alone) hi (for) aatmanah (one's) bandhuh (friend), aatma (one self) eva (alone) ripuh (enemy) aatmanah (one's).

Translation

One should lift oneself by one self above the body/mind/intellect complex, because all these belong to matter. May, one not degrade or destroy oneself. For this self is one's benefactor when there is the acceptance that there is no need for mundane things such as the body/mind/intellect complex in spiritual growth. He alone is his enemy when he accepts affinity with the body/mind/intellect complex.

217

Bondage and Liberation takes place in the Manas (Mind)

Amrtabindu Upanisad verse 2 informs us, that both bondage and liberation take place in the manas (mind):

Manah eva manusyaanaam, kaaranam bandha moksayoh; bandhaya visayaasaktam, muktam nirvisayam smrtam.

Manah (the mind) eva (alone) manusyam (of human beings) karanam (is the cause) bandha (of bondage) muksayoh (and freedom),

bandhaya (for bondage) visayaasaktam (attached to the sense objects) muktam (free) nirvisayam (devoid of desires for objects) smrtam (is considered).

Translation

This human mind alone, is the cause of bondage and freedom from limitations. Immersion of the mind (manas) in senory pursuits, is the cause of bondage i.e. the cycle of birth and death (samsara). A mind (mana) detached (vairagya) from sensory pursuits and which is focussed on seeking to experience its eternal position, will gain freedom from limitations (moksha).

Translation adapted.

Aastaavakra Gita 1:11 is supportive of the notion that bondage and freedom are mental concepts as follows:

218

Muktaa bhimaani mukto hi, baddho baddha abhimanyapi;
kim-vadanteeh satyeyam, yaa matih saa gatir-bhavet.

Mukta-abhimani (one who considers himself free) mukta (is free) hi (certainly), baddha-abhimaani (one who considers himself bound) baddhah (becomes bound).

Translation

One who considers himself free is free. One who considers himself bound is bound.

A weak mind (manas) follows the senses (indriyas) wherever they go

The mind (manas), is meant to be the master of the senses, but because they (the senses) are created as outgoing by nature the internal Self/Soul (Aatma) is missed Kathapanisad 2;4:1 is very clear on this point:

Paraanci khani vyatrnat svayambhuh, tasmaat paraan pashyati na antaraatman;

Kashcid dheerah pratyag aAatmaanam aiksat, aavrtta caksur amrtatvam icchan.

Paraanchi (outward going) khani (the sense organs) vyatrnat (masde them) svayambhooh (The self created Lord),

tasmat (that is why) paraan (things outside) pashyati (sees only things) na (not) antaraAatman (the internal self);
kashchit (some) dhirah (wise person) pratyag (within) aAatmaanam (the self) eksat(sees),
avrtta (turned inside) chaksuh (eyes) amrtatvam (immortality) iccha (wishing to get).

Translation

The Self -created Lord made the sense organs with inherent defects i.e. they are outgoing; therefore, living beings see the external universe and not the internal aatma (Self / Soul). A wiseman desirous of immortality can with draw his senses from the external world and turn within whereupon, he will experience the self.

Additional Translation

The aatma (Self /Soul) is the master of ksetram (the body/mind/intellect/complex). It is within this ksetram (body/mind/intellect complex); it is eternal and is our real nature. It can only be experienced if one has an irrestible desire to do so; to accomplish this, the senses have to be mastered so that they can be made to turn within to gain this experience.

Since this ksetram (body/mind/intellect) may not last until tomorrow, as death is in active pursuit of it, it is very important that the inward journey begins as a matter of importance. The finite nature of ksetram (the body/mind/intellect complex) is made clear by Kathopanisad 1:1:26

Shvobhaava martyasya yad antakaitat, sarven-driyaanaam jarayanti tejah.

Shvo (tomorrow) abhaavaah (not lasting) martasya (of the mortal man) yat (all these) antaka (O death) etat (all this); Sarva (all) indriyaanaam (the senses) jarayanti (exhaust) tejah (vigour).

Translation of Kathopanisad 1:1:26

O death no one knows whether the body/mind/intellect complex (ksetram) will last until tomorrow. Pursuit of the transitory exhausts the vigour of the individual and leads to decay.

The Mind (mana) bondage (bandha) and Liberation (moksha)

As long as the mind (manasa) is free to roam in the external world of sense objects, the embodied living being (jiva), will always be influenced by the his/her internal enemies resulting in suffering. These enemies are:

- Kama – (desire).

- Krodhah – (anger).

- Lobha – (greed).

221

- Moha – (delusion).

- Mada – (envy)

- Matsarya - (pride)

- Ragas – (likes/attachments).

- Dvesas – (dislikes/hatred)

Manas (the mind) is difficult to control

Gita 6:34 and 6:35 reminds us about difficulties in controlling manas (the mind). i) Gita 6:34 and Gita 6:.35 provides the following guidance:

1) Gita 6:34

Cancalam hi manah krsna, pramaathi balavad drdham;

tasyaaham nigraham manye, vaayor iva su-duskaram.

Canchalam (agitated or flickering) hi (indeed) manah (mind) Krsna (O Krishna), pramaathi (agitating) bala-vat (strong) drdham (well rooted and obstinate);
tasya (its) aham (I) nigraham (control) manye (think), vayoh (the wind) iva (like) su-duskaram (difficult).

222

Translation

As we all know, the mind is flickering, strong, obstinate and I think of it, as being more difficult to control than the wind.

2) Gita 6:35

Mano durnigraham calam, abhaayasena tu kaunteya, vairaagyena ca grhyate.

Manah (the mind) durnigraham (difficult to control) calam (flickering), abhyasena (by practice) tu (but) Kaunteya (O son of Kunti), vairagyena (by detachment) ca (also) grhyate (can be controlled).

Translation

The flickering mind is difficult to control, O son of Kunti; but with appropriate practice and detachment, it can be brought under control.

Suggestions for gaining mastery of the mind (manah)

The knowledge that each embodied living being (jiva), is a fragment (amsha) of The Supreme (Param) Lord (Aatma) and that each fragment (amsha) is eternal, has to take place in the mind (manah). Earlier, it was mentioned that our minds, were subjected to the influence of our internal enemies thus making it very difficult to control.

223

Some suggestions for gaining mastery of the mind (manah) are:

1) Anugraha -The Grace of The Lord is needed

Our religious books (shastras) advises the spiritual aspirant (sadhaka), to invoke the Grace of The Lord, before commencing on a journey of purification (shuddhi) of the mind (antah karana) in order, to remove all obstacles towards gaining mastery.

2) Sarangathi -surrender unconditionally to The Lord

Gita 18:66 provides the following guidance on how to surrender:

Sarva-dharmaan parityajya, maam ekam sharanam vrja;

aham tvam sarva-paapebyo, moksayisyaami maa shucah.

Sarva (all) dharmam (varieties of religion) parityajya (give up/abandon), mam (me) ekam (only) sharanam (refuge) vraja (take/seek);

aham (I) tvam (you) sarva (all) papebhyah (from all sinful reactions), moksayisyami (shall free) maa (do not) shucha (grieve).

Translation

Abandon all varieties of religious practice and, surrender only to me. I will free you from all sinful reactions; do not grieve.

Additional Translation

The lord is advising, the performance of selfless action (niskaama karma), in an attitude of renouncing the fruits of efforts (karma phala tyaga) and dedicating the work and their fruits to Him (Vishnu arpanam astu).

Gita 9:22 reveals that those who worship The Lord alone, will have **their unrealized needs met by Him and, he will protect what they have.**

Those who surrender the Self/Soul (aatma) to the lotus feet of The Lord, will be freed of all their defects.

3) Viveka (discrimination)

What is Viveka (discrimination)?

Swami Tejomayananda (2001) explains viveka (discrimination) as the ability or capacity of the buddhi (intellect) to identify, list and recognize one object from another. Soanes and Hawker (2008) sees viveka (discrimination) as recognition of the difference between one thing and another. Swami Harshananda (1995) defines viveka (discrimination) as the ability to know the difference between the real and the unreal.

Examples of viveka (discrimination)

The ability to recognize the difference between the following:

a) Absolute existence i.e. The Lord (Sat) and impermanent existence the world (asat)

b) The Aatma (Self/Soul) is non-different from Paramatma (The Lord) and is permanent whereas, the ksetram (body/mind/intellect complex is subject to decay and death thus, it is impermanent.

c) Nitya (eternal) and anitya (non-eternal).

d) Dharma (virtuous conduct) and adharma (non-virtuous conduct).

4) Vairagya (detachment)

Definition of Vairagya (detachment)

According to Swami Harshananda (1995) vairagya (detachment) is the giving up of all the objects of pleasure. Swami Dayananda Saraswati (1997) goes further by adding, that it is an attitude of detachment for objects of this world and the hereafter.

Attachment to this world is a barrier to spiritual progress

Attachment (sambandhah) to this world (loka) is a barrier, to spitiual progress; Some examples of attachment are:

- Ratim - pleasures.

- Grham - home.

- Kulam or gotram - family.

- Dhanam - wealth.

- Ksetram - body-mind-intellect complex.

Some Examples of Vairagya (detachment) are:

a) Withdrawal of the mind (Manah) from external pursuits

Gita 6:25 provides the following guidance:

Shanaih shanair uparamed, buddhya dhrti-grheetaya;

aatma samstham manah kritva, na kincid api cintayet.

Shanaih (gradually) shanair (step by step) uparamed (one should withdraw), buddhya (with the intellect) dhrti (perseverance) grhitayaa (endowed with);

aatma (the self) samstham (placed) manah (the mind) krtva (making), na (not) kincit (anything) api (else) cintayet (may one think of).

Translation

One should withdraw one's mind gradually, in a step by step fashion, from external pursuits, with perseverance and understanding, fixing the mind on the aatma (Self/Soul) alone and, not think about anything else.

227

b) Maximise this rare human birth to gain Aatma (Self) Vidya (knowledge)

Among various living creatures (jantum) in this world (jagat), this human (nara) birth (janma) is difficult to obtain (durlabham). To have a human (nara) birth (janma) and to possess manly qualities eg courage, sacrifice and renunciation, is very rare (durlabham). Only in this human (nara) birth (janma) alone, does one have the opportunity, to gain knowledge (vidya) of the Self/Soul i.e. we are not the body-mind-intellect-complex (ksetram) but we are the Self/Soul which is non-different form the Lord.

c) Give up this time bound world

The real you (Self/Soul-aatma) exists, within this body-mind-intellect complex (ksetram), as The Lord within (Antaryami). In order to experience one's real nature (The Self /Soul - aatma), it is essential to withdraw the mind from this time bound (mithya) world (jagat) and turn within.

d) Walking the road of the good (Shreyas)

Walking the road of the good (shreyas) and conducting one's self in a virtuous (dharmik), truthful (sat), loving (prema) and peaceful (shanti) manner is advised, as it purifies the mind (manah).

e) Performing selfless service (niskama karma)

Acts of selfless service (niskama karma), without the expectation of a reward (karma phala tyaga) and

228

dedicating the work and its reward to the Lord (Vishnu arpanam astu) also purifies the mind.

f) <u>Be guided by the Religious Books (Shastras)</u>

Allow the religious books (shastras) to be your guide. Make friends with them.

g) <u>Live like a tenant in this world</u>

Live like a tenant in this world (jagat); remember, tenancy has a beginning and an end. Do not not get attached to I (aham) and mine (mama) because, they bind one to the world of transmigration (samsara) which is a waste, of this rare human (nara) birth (janma).

5) <u>Group of six (Shamadi-satka)</u>

This group is made up of the following:

a) Shama -mental tranquillity

<u>What is Shama?</u>

Shama is the tranquillity of the mind, brought about by constant practice of keeping it from roaming in the external world of sensory objects.

<u>Benefits of Shama</u>

Shama or mental tranquillity, frees the mind of impurities such as restlessness and passion (rajas) and, laziness and ignorance (tamas) which it gains from the world of the senses.

Some exercises to gain shama (mental tranquillity)

- Prarthna (Prayers).
- Japa (Repitition of The Lord's name (s).
- Shastric study (reading, reflecting and living the message of the scriptures)
- Thinking (bhavana) positive (paksa) instead of negative (prati).

b) Dama (Subjagation of the senses)

What is dama (subjugation of the senses)?

Restraint of the senses (dama) is the control of the five (panch) organs of knowledge (jnana indriyas) and five (panch) organs of action (karma indriyas).

The five (panch) organs of Knowledge (jnana indriyas) are:

- Ear (strotram).
- Eyes (chaksu).
- Nose (grhnam).
- Tongue (rasana).
- Skin (tvak).

The five (panch) organs of action (karma indriyas) are:

- Speech (vak).

- Hands (pani).

- Legs (pada).

- Genitals (upasthani).

- Anus (payu).

Some exercises to gain control of the senses (dama)

- See no evil, hear no evil, speak no evil and do no evil.

- Practice allowing your ears to hear the transcendental glories and pastimes of the Lord in all sounds.

- Strive to see The Lord in everyone and everything you look at.

- Let each breath remind you that you are The Lord (So- The Lord), ham- (I am).

- Let your words always be truthful (Satyam), auspicious (shivam), beautiful (sundaram), sweet (madhuram) and blissful (anandam).

- Utilise the whole body, to provide selfless service (niskama karma), in a spirit of non-expectation of a reward (karma-phala-tyaga) and dedicating the action and its rewards to The Lord (Vishnu arpanam astu).

c) Uparati (removal of one's self from stimuli which disturbs the mind)

Removal of one's self from stimuli, which disturbs one's mental equilibrium (uparati) is an aid to spiritual growth.

Exercises to develop one's Uparati

- Provision of selfless service (niskama karma) to one's parents, siblings, family, local community, country and the world.

- Association with devotees of The Lord (satsanga) and a good environment uplifts and purifies the mind.

- Reduce your dependence on sensory objects and increase your desire for spiritual growth.

- Develop a desire for fasting (vrata) as it quietens and steadies the mind.

- Chant the name (s) of The Lord (japa) orally or mentally as this gains the grace of The Lord (anugraha).

d) Titiksa (endurance)

What is Titiksa (endurance)?

Titiksa (endurance) is the cheerful acceptance, of what comes our way, as the Grace of The Lord (anugraha), always (nityam) accepting with an even mind (sama citta tvam) these pairs of opposites.

Some examples of what comes our way or the pairs of opposites

- Praise and blame.

- Love and hate.

- Success and failure.

- Wealth and poverty.

- Health and ill health.

- Happiness and unhappiness.

- Heat and cold.

The ideal approach to deal with the pairs of opposites

- Do not get elated when praised nor dejected when blamed.

- The pairs of opposites are time bound i.e. they have a beginning and an end. Do not get attached to them.

233

- See blame, hate, failure, poverty, ill health, unhappiness as opportunities to advance your spiritual growth

e) Shraddha (faith)

What is Shraddha (faith)?

It is having total confidence in the shastra (scripture), the acharya (teacher) and in Paramatma (The Lord).

Gita 4:39 and shraddha (faith)

Shraddhavan labhate jnaanam

Shraddhavan (a faithful person) labhate (gains) jnanam (Knowledge)

Translation

A faithful person gains knowledge.

f) Samadhana (concentration)

What is Samadhana (concentration)?

This is the total ability to fix manah (the mind) on the aatma (Self/Soul) at all times.

6) Mumuksatva (desire for liberation)

What is mumuksutva (desire for liberation)?

It is an intense longing and desire, to break free, from the cycle of birth (janma), growth (vardhanam), disease (vyadhi), defects (dosa), pain (duhkham), old age (jara) and death (mrtyu).

References

Chaitanya S (1993) - Tattva Bodha of Sankaracarya - C C M T, Mumbai, 400 072, India – P:17.

Swami Chinmayananda (1997) - Astavakra Gita - C C M T, Mumbai, 400 072, India -1:11.

Swami Chinmayananda (1998) - Aparokshanubhuti (Intimate experience of reality)- C C M T, Mumbai, 400 072, India – Verse 9.

Swami Chinmayananda (2000) -Kathopanisad (A Dialogue with death) - C C M T, Mumbai, 400 072, India - 2:41, 1:1:26.

Swami Harshananda (1995) - A Dictionary of Advaita Vedanta - Ramakrishna Math, Bangalore, 560 019, India.

Swami Lokeswarananda (2009) - Katha Upanisad - Ramakrishna Mission Institute of Culture, Kolkata 700 029, India – 2:41, 1:1:26.

Swami Lokeswarananda (2010) - Chandogya Upanisad - Ramakrishna Mission Institute of Culturem, Kolkata, 700 029, India - 8:12:5

Nath P. V. (2002) - Tat Tvam Asi (The Universal Message in The Bhagavadgita) - Motilal Banarsidas, Delhi, 110 007, India - 6:5, 6:34, 6:35, 18:66, 9:22, 6:2

Swami Prabhupada (1985) - The Bhagavadgita (As it is) - Bhaktivedanta Book Trust, Watford, WD2 4XA, Herts, UK - 6:34, 6:35.

Swami Ramsukhdas (2005) -Srimad Bhagavadgita (Sadhaka Sanjivini) - Gita Press, Gorakhpur, 270 005, UP, India - 6:5, 6:34, 6:35, 18:66, 9:22, 6:25.

Swami Dayananda Saraswati (1997) - Vivekacudamani (Talks on 108 Selected Verses) - Sri Gangadharesvar Trust, Rishikesh, 249 201, U. P, India -Verses2-3.

Swami Dayananda Saraswati (2004) - Tattva Bodhah - Arsha Vidya Gurukulum, Coimbatore, Tamil Nadu641 108, India – P:11.

Swami Dayananda Saraswati (2006) - Bhagavadgita (Home Study Coures) - Arsha Vidya Gurukulum, Coimbatore, Tamil Nadu, 641 108, India - 6:5, 6:34, 6:35, 6:25, 2:4:39.

Soanes C. (2008) - Compact Oxford English Dictionary - Oxford University Press, Oxford University, Oxford, U. K.

Swami Suddhabodhananda (1994) -Panchadashi (Tattva Viveka)- Sri Visweswar Trust, Bombay, 400 056, India – Chap 1: Verse 20.

Swami Tejomayananda (2001) - Tattva Bodhah (Shri Aadi Shankaracharya- CCMT, Mumbai, 400 072, India – P :12.

Swami Tejomayananda (2010) - Amritabindu Upanisad - CC MT, Mumbai, 400 072, India - Verse 2: P:14

13

The Hindu (Sanatanist) Calender and Spiritual Growth

The Hindu (Sanatanist) calendar is an invaluable aid, to the spiritual growth of practitioner of our religion, as it provides information of religious events and their significance.

Here is a resume of important events and their importance.

1) Amavasya

What is Amavasya?

Ama = together

Vasya = to dwell

Amasvasya   to dwell together.

Amavasya is referred to as:

No moon or new moon.

Spiritual significance of Amavasya

- It is an auspicious time, to seek the blessings of our ancestors, for their contributions, to our progress so far.

- It is a time to be charitable to all members of The Lord's creation.

- This is the time to fast (vrat) in order to gain mastery of the mind (manas) and the senses (dama) in order to aid our spiritual growth.

2) Pradosh Vrat

What is Pradosh?

Pradosh means evening.

What is Vrat

Vrat refers to fasting.

Spiritual significance of Pradosh Vrat

This is the most auspicious time, to pray to Lord Shiva and Parvati Mata, to gain:

- Freedom from limitations (moksha).

- Success in all of our daily activities of living.

- Children who are in the mode of goodness (sattva),

3) Purnima

What is Purnima?

Purnima is referred to as full moon.

Spitiual significance of Purnima

- It is a time to give thanks, to all the **avatars** (descent of The Lord into the material world) of Lord Vishnu for His role in perpetuating our welfare and development.

- This is a time of praying, fasting and meditating to gain the grace (anugraha) of The Lord, to aid in our spiritual growth,

4) Guru Purnima

What is Guru Purnima?

It is the time to remember our individual spiritual master (acharya) and our universal spiritual master (Lord Shiva), for waking us from our sleep of ignorance (avidya) to the reality that we are the aatma (Self/Soul) and, that aatma (Self/Soul) is non- different from Paramatma (The Lord).

Maharishi Veda Vyasa

At this period, we are encouraged to rememember with thanks, the gift of Maharishi Veda Vyasa to us from God; his gifts to us are:

- The four Vedas - Rg, Yajur, Sama and Atharva.
- Eighteen (18) Puranas.
- Mahabharata.
- Shrimad Bhagavatam.

This is a time to:

- Reflect on our spiritual progress, thus far and to map the way forward to this continued growth.

- Continue with our fasting (vrat), prayer (prarthna) and meditation (dhyanam) to aid our spiritual growth.

5) Vasant Panchami

What is Vasant Panchami?

It is the festival of spring.

What is the significance of Vasant Panchami?

This is the occasion when plants and trees, bloom with flowers and fruits and the animal kingdom is joyful.

Spiritual significance of Vasant Panchami

- Give thanks to mother earth (Prthvi Mata), for bearing us with dignity and providing us with all of our nutritional needs.

- Express our appreciation to Saraswati Mata (The Lord's expression of knowledge) for the provision of our educational needs.

6) Maha Shivratri?

What is Maha Shivratri?

Maha (great)

Shiva (an expression of The Lord of the universe).

Ratri (night). Maha Shivratri is the great night of Lord Shiva

Spiritual significance of Maha Shiv Ratri

- It is the day of the marriage of Lord Shiva (an expression of The Lord) and Parvati (The universal mother).

- He (Lord Shiva) appeared to his pious devotees as The Lord with attributes (saguna brahman) on this day in order to please and give kinship to them.

- During this time, he consumed the poison which originated from churning of kshir (milk) sagar (ocean), for the benefit of the world.

- Devotees fast (vrat), pray (prarthna) and chant (kirthanam) The Lord's name (s) to strengthen their spiritual growth.

7) Holi

What is Holi?

Holi is defined as:

- The festival of spring.

- The reduction of evil to ashes.

- Festival of colours.

Origination of the word Holi

Holi is the term which originated from **Holika,** the name of the sister of the demon king - Hiranyakasipu (The father of Prahalada).

Brief account of Holi

Prahalada (the son of the demon king Hiranyakasipu), was a devout devotee of The Lord of the world (Vishnu). His father proclaimed himself as God but, he (Prahalada) recognized only Vishnu as The Lord of the world. Try as he may, Hiranyakasipu failed to be recognized as God by his son.

Out of frustration, he decided to end the life of his son, so he tricked his son Prahalada to sit on his aunt's lap on a huge fire. His aunt Holika was supposed to be immune from being burnt as she was wearing a fire proof coat.

As the fire roared, the Lord made it possible for the fire-resistant coat, to be transferred from Holika to Prahalada thus, Holika was incinerated to ashes and Prahalada was saved.

Spiritual significance of Holi

- Firm faith (shraddha) in The Lord enables the devotee (bhakta) to overcome evil.
- Evil is reduced to ashes.
- This an ideal time to re-affirms one's faith in God.

8) Ramnaumi

What is Ramnaumi?

Ramnaumi is the descent (avatara) of Shri Rama (the 7th incarnation) of The Lord of the world (Vishnu).

Purpose of The Lord's descent (avatara)

The purpose of The Lord's descent (avatara) into this mataerial world, was designed to re-establish:

- The religion of truth (Satya)
- Virtuous conduct (Dharma).
- Give kinship to His devotees.
- Motivate them to continue with their spiritual growth.

Rama - the role model

As a role model Shri Rama was:

- An ideal son who was very respectful and loving.
- An ideal brother who was always loving and caring.
- An ideal husband who loved and protected His wife.
- An ideal king who promoted the welfare of His subjects.
- An embodiment of compassion, gentleness, kindness, righteousness and integrity.

- A perfect person (maryada Purushottama)

Spiritual significance to the devotee

- Reflect on the above roles that are appropriate to us and seek room for improvement (s).

- Re-examine our transaction with external world and seek to make this virtuous, peaceful and loving.

- Seek to maximise our allotted lifespan in the provision of activities to promote the welfare of all,

9) Navratri

What is Navratri?

Nava-(nine).

Ratri – (nights).

What happens at Navaratri?

During Navaratri (nine nights), The Divine mother of the world, though one, is worshipped in her expressions as Durga, Lakshmi and Saraswati.

What happens in the first three (3) nights?

The Divine mother is worshipped in her expression as Durga, in order to:

- Grace us with noble qualities.

- Destroy our inner enemies e.g. attachments (ragas), dislikes/hatred (dvesas), desires (kama), anger (krodhaha), greed (lobha), delusions (moha), pride (mada) and envy (matsarya) so that we come to realize that the Self/ Soul (aatma) and The Lord (Paramatma) are one and the same.

What happens during the second (2) three (3) nights

The Divine mother is worshipped in her expression as Lakshmi, to grace us with a mind that is pure, concentrated, controlled and single focus, so that it can be receptive to the knowledge that we are the aatma (Self/Soul) and it is non-different from Paramatma (The Lord)

What happens in the last three (3) nights

Now that our minds are pure, they are receptive to the fact that, we are the aatma (Self/ Soul) and not this body-mind-intellect system (ksetram) and that, this aatma (Self/Soul) and Paramatma (The Lord) are one and the same. We pray to Saraswati Mata (the knowledge expression of The Lord) to grace us with this knowledge.

<u>What happens on the tenth (10) day of navaratri</u>

The tenth (10th) day of Nauratri (nine nights) is called **Vijaya Dashmi.** On this day, the impurities of the mind have been replaced by virtuous values and aatma (Self) vidya (knowledge) i.e. we are the aatma (Self/Soul) and, it is non-different from Paramatma (The Supreme Lord).

10) <u>Hanuman Jayanti</u>

<u>What is Hanuman Jayanti?</u>

Hanuman Jayanti is the day When Lord Shiva (an expression of Lord of the world - Vishnu), descended into this material world (avatar) to aid Shri Rama (the 7th Avatar of the Lord of the world -Vishnu) in his objective of re-establishing;

- The religion of truth (Satya).

- Virtuous conduct (Dharma).

<u>Spiritual significance of Hanuman Jayanti)</u>

- It is a time to surrender the mind (Hanuman) to the Self/Soul (Rama).

- It is an opportunity to recommit ourselves to the pursuit of aatma (Self/Soul) vidya (knowledge) i.e. the aatma (Self/Soul) and Paramatma (The lord) are one and the same and, this is permanent whereas, the ksetram (body-mind-intellect complex) is impermanent.

- A reminder that chanting the Hanuman Chalisa, purifies the mind thus making it receptive for aatma (Self/Soul) vidya (knowledge) i.e. we are aatma (Self/Soul) which is non-different from Paramatma (The Lord).

11) Sita Jayanti

What is Sita Jayanti?

Sita Jayanti is the descent (avatar), of Lakshmi Mata (mother Lakshmi - the resource expression of The Lord), in to this material world, for the purpose, of aiding Her consort - Shri Rama (The 7th avatar of Vishnu) in achieving the objective of His descent into this material world.

Spiritual significance of Sita Jayanti

- To motivate spiritual aspirant (sadhaka) to strengthen their spiritual growth.

- To act as a role model for women.

12) Raksha Bandhan

What is Raksha Bandhan?

Raksha- protection

Bandhan - bond of

Raksha Bandhan is the tying of the knot of affection.

Significance of Raksha Bandhan

- It is a symbol of love.

- It is the obligation of the strong to protect the weak.

- It is re-inforcement of family values.

What happens on this day?

- Sisters tie a a thread or band (rakhee) on the right wrist of their brothers.

- Sisters pray for their borther's protection.

- Brothers give gifts to their sisters.

13) Ganesh Chaturthi

What is Ganesh Chaturthi?

Ganesh Chaturthi is the day on which Shri Ganesh (an expression of the Lord of the world) descended (avatar) into this material world

Ganesh, Riddhi and Siddhi

Shri Ganesh is married to Riddhi (prosperity) and Siddhi (attainment), both of which are daughters of Prajapati (the protector of humankind).

Role of Shri Ganesh

- Remover of obstacles to spiritual and material progress.
- Giver of intelligence.
- Brings and unite people together.
- Lord of wisdom, arts and literature.
- Lord of new beginnings. His blessings are sought before commencement of:
  1. A marriage.
  2. An Examination.
  3. Building of a house.
  4. A business.
  5. Going for an interview.
  6. A journey.

Spiritual Significance of Ganesh Chaturthi

- Aids successful spiritual growth.

14) Pitr Paksh

What is Pitr Paksh?

Pitr (ancestors).

Paksh (a particular time).

Pitr Paksh - is a time to perform religious ritual (shraadha) and donate food and water, in memory of our ancestors. It is called the fornight of our ancestors.

It is a time to:

Demonstrate gratitude and Give thanks to our ancestors for their contributions, for the richness of life we now enjoy.

15) Janam Ashtami

What is Janam ashtami?

Janam ashtami is the day when Shri Krishna (the 8th descent of the Lord of the world) incarnated or appeared in our material world.

Purpose of Shri Krishna's appearance in our material world

- To foster love (prema).
- To promote peace (shanti).
- To remind us that the aatma (Self/Soul) which is within us is non differenJ from the Paramatma (Supreme Lord). We are reminded that we should turn within, to experience it.

Spiritual significance of the Lord's appearance at midnight

- He appeared at midnight, to spiritually illumine us to turn within to experience the aatma (Self/Soul).

16) Diwali

What is Diwali?

Diwali is made up of two words:

Deep (Light).

Avali (row).

Diwali refers to a row of lights.

Spirtual significance of Diwali

It is an occasion to:

- Seek to gain mastery of the mind (shama) and senses (dama), so that they aid in our spiritual growth.

- To provide selfless service (niskama karma) without expectation of reward (karma-phala-tyaga) to all members of The Lord's creation and dedicating the service to The Lord (Vishnu-arpanam-astu) in order to gain purity of mind (antah-karana-shuddhi) which is necessary for spiritual growth.

- Seek the grace (anugraha) of Divine mother Lakshmi so that we can turn within to experience our real nature i.e. the aatma (Self/Soul).

- Though our houses are well lit on this day, our hearts and minds are in total darkness.

17) Gita Jayanti

What is Gita Jayanti?

Gita Jayanti marks the day, on which Shri Krishna (the 8th incarnation or the appearance of The Lord of the world - Vishnu), delivered the Srimad Bhagavadgita to His disciple and friend (Arjuna), on the first day of the Eighteen (18) day Mahabharata war on the battlefield of Kurukshetra.

Spirtiual significance of the Shrimad Bhagavadgita

- It is a yoga shastra i.e. it brings the union of the aatma (Self/Soul) with The Paramatma (Supreme Lord).

- It is Brahma (The lord's) vidya (knowledge of).

- The Shrimad Bhagavadgita informs us that we aatma (The Self/Soul) is one without a second (advaita).

254

- It informs us of the following mahavakya (great statement):

Tat (That - The Lord) **tvam** (the Soul/Self) **asi** (art) i.e. The Lord and the Self/Soul are one and the same.

18) Kartik snana

What is kartik snana?

Commemorates the descent of Ganga Mata, from the feet of Shri Vishnu (The Lord of the world) during the month of kartik (Oct/Nov).

Spiritual Significance of Kartik snana

- It is understood that on this day, all the waters of the rivers, seas and oceans, contain the same qualities of Mother Ganga.

- A bath in a river, sea or ocean at this time makes the body-mind- intellect (ksetram) pure (antah-karana shuddhi), thus, it (the body-mind-intellect-ksetram) is receptive to aatma (Self/Soul) Vidya (knowledge) i.e. aatma (The Self/Soul) and Paramatma (The Lord) are one and the same.

19) Makar Sankranti

What is Makar Sankranti?

Makar Sankranti is the time when the sun (Surya) enters the sign of Makara (Capricorn) on 14th January (in English calendar). It usually falls in the month of Magha (in Hindu calendar).

Spirtual significance of Makar Sankranti

Though there is Sankranti in every month, the sun (surya) in Makar (Capricorn) is the ideal time to gain merit (punya) by:

1. Giving danam (charity) to the poor and the needy.

2. Bathing in the river.

3. Offering water to Lord Surya (the sun).

Bibliographies

Arjun S. H - (1983) - Hindu Dharma (Devotional Prayers and Rites) - Sharada Press, Mangalore, 571 001, India.

Hosein T and Mathura K - (1991) - Discourses by Bhagavan Sri Satya Sai Baba - The Sri Satya Sai Baba Organization, Trinidad, West Indies.

Swami Harshananda (2000) - Hindu Symbols (Including emblems and sacred objects) - Ramakrishna Math, Bangalore, 560 019, India.

Jairam B (1993) - Golden Ages of Hinduism Dharmik Prakash - Dharmik Books, W.H. Inc., Canada.

Swami Nityananda (1996) - Symbolism in Hinduism - C. C. M. T, Mumbai, 400 072, India.

Swami Tejomayananda (1995) - Hindu Culture (An Introduction) - C C M.T, Mumbai, 400 072, India,

31648184R00153

Printed in Poland
by Amazon Fulfillment
Poland Sp. z o.o., Wrocław